Warner

Baseball Card

FIELD GUIDE

MICKEY MANTLE
Mickey Mantle

Edited by Rocky Landsverk

©2004 by Krause Publications, Inc.

Published by

kp **krause publications**
An F+W Publications Company

700 East State Street • Iola, WI 54990-0001
715-445-2214 • 888-457-2873
www.krause.com

Our toll-free number to place an order or obtain
a free catalog is (800) 258-0929.

Library of Congress Catalog Number: 2004100733
ISBN: 0-87349-837-2

Edited by Rocky Landsverk

Printed in the United States of America

Baseball Cards Through The Years

Baseball cards are as American as apple pie, but in relative terms, they're a lot younger, too. It's been only 115 years or so that baseball player photographs have appeared on cardboard, giving us our first "baseball cards." In 1887, Goodwin & Co. of New York City used studio photos about 1-1/2 inches tall by 2-1/2 inches wide, glued onto stiff cardboard. These were inserted into cigarette packages with such exotic names as Old Judge, Gypsy Queen and Dogs Head. Poses were formal, with artificial backgrounds and barehanded players fielding balls suspended on strings to simulate action. While they carry the moniker "baseball cards," they were certainly a world apart from today's technologically advanced breed.

An Old Judge tobacco card from the 1880s.

Following Goodwin's lead a year later, competitors began issuing baseball cards with their cigarettes, using full-color lithography to bring to life painted portraits of the era's top players. After a few short years of stiff competition, monopolies in the tobacco industry took away that competitive spirit and left no reason for companies to produce baseball cards by the mid-1890s. The importing of Turkish tobaccos in the years just prior to 1910 rejuvenated the practice.

WAGNER, PITTSBURG

A near-perfect specimen of this T206 Honus Wagner card sold for $1.265 million.

In the years from 1909-1912, dozens of different sets of cards were produced for cigarette packages. They came in a variety of sizes, some as large as 5 by 8 inches, and collectors today call them by such names as "T206" for no reason other than hobby pioneer Jefferson Burdick gave them that designation decades ago when he was compiling the first-ever baseball card catalog.

There were Double Folders, featuring two players

on the same card, and Triple Folders, which had two player portraits and one action scene. The most famous and valuable card in the hobby – a T206 Honus Wagner card – came from this era. Because fewer than 70 have been found, and because these cards are so difficult to find in pristine condition, the top specimen known has broken the all-time baseball card record several times. It sold most recently for $1.265 million in an auction in the year 2000.

The tobacco companies' efforts to sell more product using baseball player pictures spread to other products, as you would expect. Cracker Jack began including baseball cards in each box in the 1914-15 time frame. Those cards are particularly popular today because they include players from the short-lived Federal League. The association of bubble gum with baseball cards dates to the early 1930s, when rubber tree products led to the development of bubble gum. Bubble gum, and thus baseball card, production was centered in Massachusetts, where National Chicle (Cambridge) and Goudey Gum (Boston) were headquartered.

Most bubble gum cards in the early 1930s featured a square shape, about 2-1/2 inches wide. For the first time, considerable attention was paid to the backs of

the cards, where biographical details, career high-
lights and previous season statistics were presented.

In 1939, a new company entered the baseball card
market – Gum Inc. of Philadelphia. Its "Play Ball" gum
was the major supplier of baseball cards until 1941,
when World War II caused a shortage of materials
needed for both the production of bubble gum and
the printing of baseball cards.

The Topps/Bowman Era

Baseball cards reappeared following the war in the
late 1940s. The former Gum Inc. reappeared as
Bowman Gum Inc., which produced its first set in
1948 with a 48-card effort. Color was added to the
photos in 1949, and by 1951, Bowman went to a larg-
er size, 2 inches by 3-1/8 inches. Meanwhile, Leaf
Gum in Chicago produced a set from 1948-49, highlighted by a Joe DiMaggio card.

In 1952, Brooklyn-based Topps entered baseball
card manufacturing in a major way and changed the
landscape of cards forever. It's 407-card set was the
largest in history to that point, and the 2-5/8 inches
by 3-3/4 inches format was the largest offered for
over-the-counter sale. Other innovations included the
use of team logos in card design, and on the back,

Topps put career statistics in rows of lines for the first time ever. This set was highlighted by a Mickey Mantle card that is still the hobby's most-desired issue, even though Mantle had already had a card in the 1951 Bowman set.

Is this 1953 Warren Spahn Bowman card from the best set ever?

While Topps won the battle in 1952, the following year Bowman was the clear victor with what is often considered the finest baseball card set ever produced. For the first time, actual color photographs were reproduced on cards. To allow for the full impact of the new color photos to take effect, Bowman put no graphics on the front of the card. It also boosted the size to 2-1/2 by 3-3/4 inches.

This Bowman vs. Topps competition continued for five years. In late 1955, Bowman admitted defeat and was sold to Topps. In 1957, Topps established the size that is still the standard today: 2-1/2 by 3-1/2 inches. That was also the first year that Topps used full-color photos for its cards, rather than paintings or retouched black-and-white photos.

The Topps Monopoly

For the next quarter-century, Topps would remain virtually alone on the baseball card landscape. Fleer

ROY WHITE

1972 Topps: A design of the times.

issued a few sets of old-time players in the early 1960s, then in 1963 challenged Topps' standing by producing a 66-card set of current players. Topps took Fleer to court, where the validity of Topps' exclusive contracts with players was upheld. Topps would not be challenged again for almost 20 years.

The 1960s offered baseball card collecting at its purest. Youngsters would wait all winter for Topps to issue its set the following spring. When they arrived, it was a rush to the corner store to drop 5 cents per pack and check out the latest designs. Then, periodically during the summer, Topps would release new series, with the card numbering continuing from the previous series that year to create one large set. The "high numbers" series often weren't carried by the stores, as they weren't as popular late in the season, and those high-number cards are now more valuable due to scarcity.

The early 1970s brought important new developments. The decade's first two Topps releases were stunning to card collectors as the company eschewed the traditional white border for gray in 1970 and black in 1971. The designs were fairly traditional, however, which changed in 1972, when the company went wild with a psychedelic, brightly colored frame. It was certainly a sign of the times.

Another significant change occurred in 1973. Rather than distributing the cards in multiple series over the course of the spring and summer, Topps began issuing the season's cards all at once, in one large release. While that had some negative impacts for collectors who enjoyed the more quaint delivery system, it also began the era of the card dealer. Many baseball card shops got their start when the cards were available all at once. It made it easier for dealers to complete their sets earlier in the year, and thus made it easier for them to market sets as a whole to collectors. The era of the card shop was born.

Renewed Competition

By 1981, the baseball card hobby was booming, and

other companies weren't going to let Topps benefit by itself. A federal court broke Topps' monopoly on the issuing of baseball cards with bubble gum, and Topps was joined by Fleer (from Philadelphia) and Donruss (from Memphis). That same year saw the resurgence of regional baseball card issues. Over the next few years, companies producing everything from snack cakes to soda were adding cards to their packaging for more appeal. By 1984, more than half of the major league teams were issuing their own regional sets. The hobby hadn't seen so much diversity since the 1950s.

The mid-1980s continued a growth trend in the number of companies and the number of dealers and collectors. Topps was trying new technologies like oversized cards, 3-D plastic cards and metal cards. A fourth company, Sportflics, joined the fray in 1986 with three photos on each card to simulate a 3-D effect. Company No. 5, called Score, entered in 1988, and the now-famous Upper Deck Co. jumped into cards in 1989, hitting a home run with card No. 1 in its first set: Ken Griffey Jr. Upper Deck became the first – and is still the only – company to put a hologram on each card to prevent counterfeiting.

The hobby was hopping and times were good for collectors. Baseball cards were so popular that more than 100,000 people attended the National Sports Collectors Convention in Anaheim, Calif., in 1991.

Card Explosion

Both 1992 and 1993 saw more than $1 billion in card sales, and along with the popularity, cards became more expensive and fancy. Autographs started appearing on cards in packs, and companies began to issue low press run sets in hopes of driving up values and interest. The 1993 Topps Finest brand, for instance, was intentionally short-printed, driving packs up to $20 apiece on the secondary market.

The early to mid 1990s became the generation of the "insert" card. Called insert cards because they are inserted into sets at lower ratios than regular or "base" cards, inserts cards started to see elaborate technologies and autographs. "Parallel" sets were created that mirrored the regular set, but in a different color or with a special stamp, and with more scarcity. And in 1996, the memorabilia card boom began, as companies began putting pieces of game-used memorabilia like jerseys and bats onto cards. While it's become quite an area of controversy as card companies cut up jerseys, bats and the like to put pieces onto cards, card collectors have clamored for the cards ever since.

Another new trend is for companies to design their new sets like the sets of old, which creates interest from veteran collectors who remember those designs.

A Guide To This Book

In this book, we've pictured 500 baseball cards that have nothing in common except that we like them and they have some importance in baseball card collecting. We've attempted to show you some vintage cards from bygone eras; some important "rookie cards" of some of the best players in major league history; some of the newer "insert" cards, especially those featuring autographs or game-used memorabilia pieces; and some of the new generation of cards that use old-time designs on new sets.

Please keep in mind that the card prices shown are what you could expect to pay from a card dealer; you wouldn't necessarily be able to sell them for this amount. Also keep in mind that the prices shown reflect cards that are in nearly perfect condition. Cards that are dinged up or stained aren't as valuable. We hope you enjoy this trip through baseball card history, and join us as the journey continues in baseball cards.

Rocky Landsverk

Editorial Director, *Sports Collectors Digest*

Henry Aaron
1954 Topps Rookie Card
$800

Henry Aaron
1959 Bazooka
$485

Henry Aaron
1961 Topps All-Star
$85

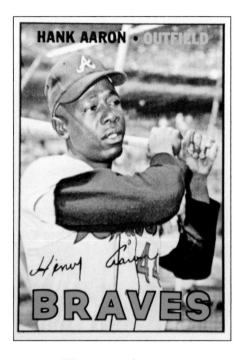

HANK AARON • OUTFIELD

BRAVES

Henry Aaron
1967 Topps
$60

HANK
AARON

LIFE GRAND SLAM

Henry Aaron
1987 Allstate Insurance
$12

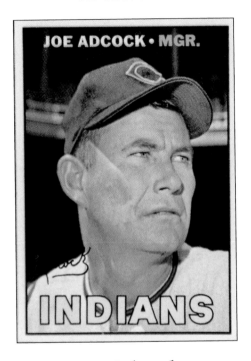

Joe Adcock
1967 Topps
$16

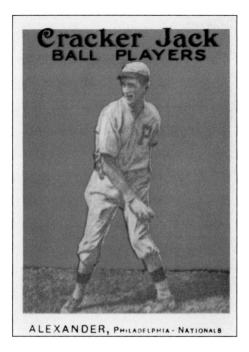

Grover Alexander
1914 Cracker Jack
$3,000

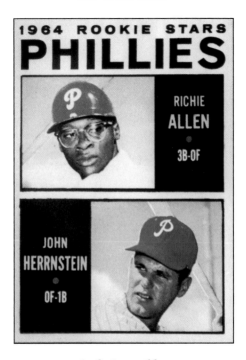

Richie Allen
1964 Topps Rookie Card
$20

Roberto Alomar
1988 Donruss Rookie Card
$1

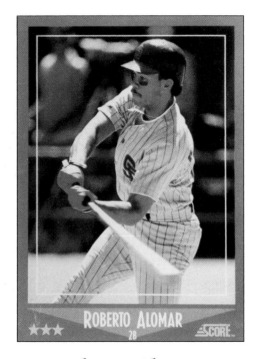

Roberto Alomar

1988 Score Traded/Rookie Card No. 105

$5

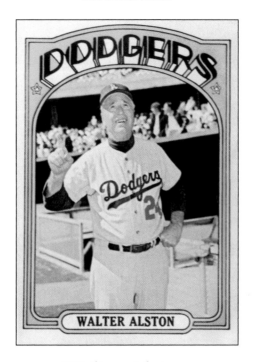

Walter Alston
1972 Topps
$11

Garret Anderson

2003 Donruss

$1

Baseball Card Field Guide

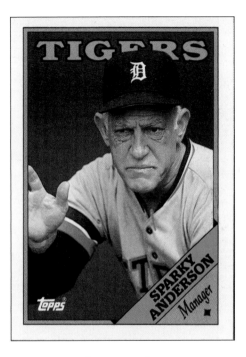

Sparky Anderson
1988 Topps
$1

ADRIAN C. ANSON.
ALLEN & GINTER'S
Cigarettes
RICHMOND. VIRGINIA.

Cap Anson
1887 Allen & Ginter World's Champions
$2,900

LUIS APARICIO
Shortstop

Chicago
White Sox

Luis Aparicio
1961 Topps
$14

JEFF BAGWELL·1B
Houston Astros

Jeff Bagwell
2003 Donruss Diamond Kings
$1

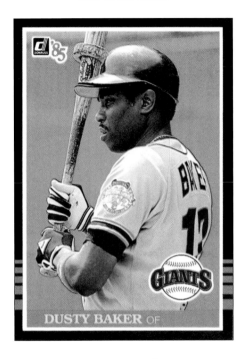

Dusty Baker
1985 Donruss
$1

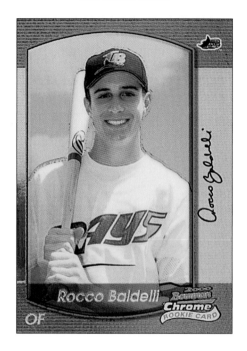

Rocco Baldelli
2000 Bowman Chrome Draft Picks & Prospects
Rookie Card
$25

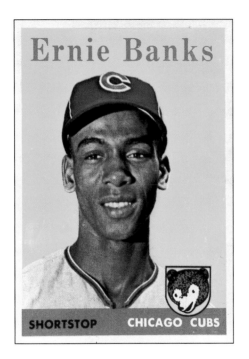

Ernie Banks
1958 Topps
$70

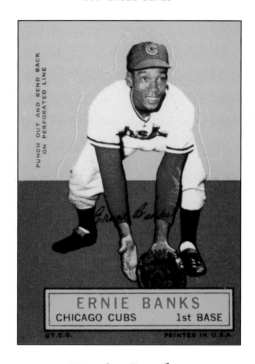

Ernie Banks
1964 Topps Stand-Ups
$80

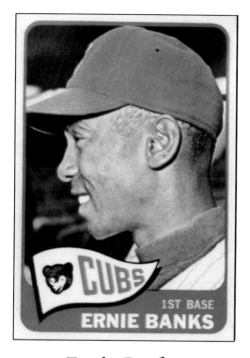

Ernie Banks
1965 Topps
$43

Josh Beckett
1999 Fleer Update No. 122
$10

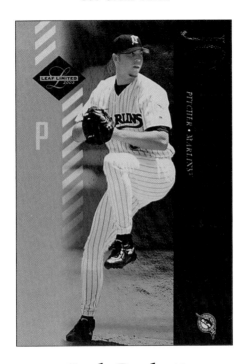

Josh Beckett

2003 Leaf Limited

$2

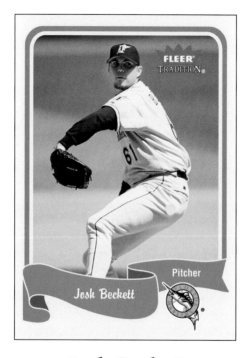

Josh Beckett

2004 Fleer Tradition

$1

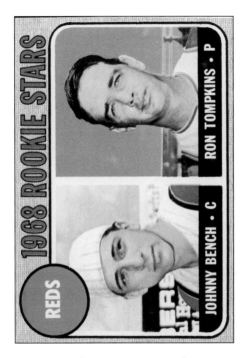

Johnny Bench
1968 Topps Rookie Card
$75

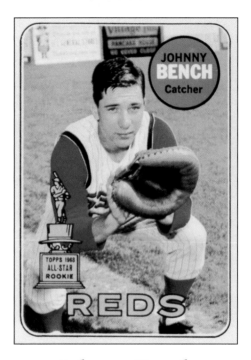

Johnny Bench
1969 Topps
$37

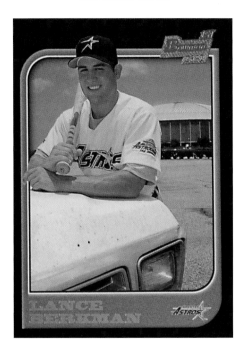

Lance Berkman
1997 Bowman Rookie Card
$2

Yogi Berra
1953 Bowman Color
$750

YOGI BERRA
Catcher-Outfield

New York
Yankees

Yogi Berra
1961 Topps
$50

Yogi Berra
1965 Topps
$38

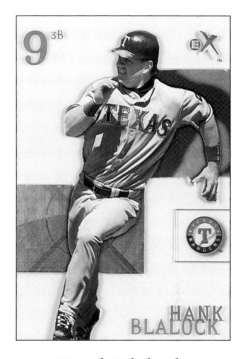

Hank Blalock
2003 Fleer E-X
$1

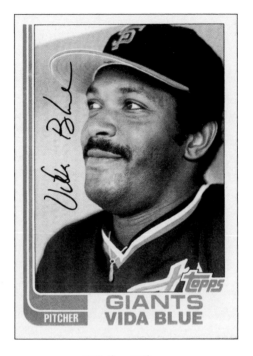

Vida Blue
1982 Topps
$1

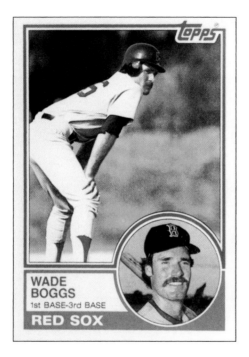

Wade Boggs
1983 Topps Rookie Card
$12

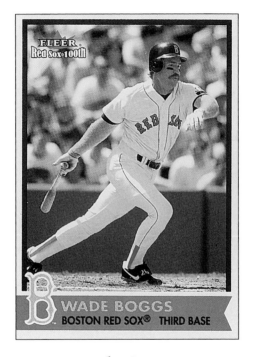

Wade Boggs

2001 Fleer Boston Red Sox 100th Anniversary

$2

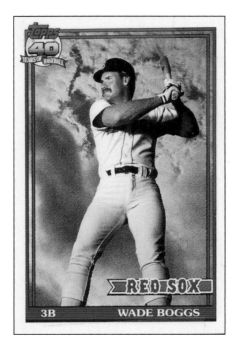

Wade Boggs
1991 Topps
$1

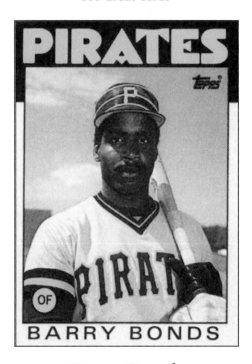

Barry Bonds
1986 Topps Traded Rookie Card
$20

Barry Bonds
1987 Fleer
$35

Barry Bonds
1993 Topps Finest
$8

Barry Bonds
2003 Topps Total
$2

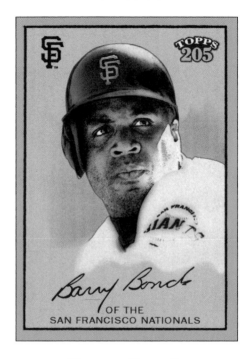

Barry Bonds
2003 Topps205
$3

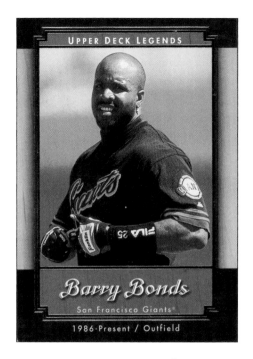

Barry Bonds
2001 Upper Deck Legends
$3

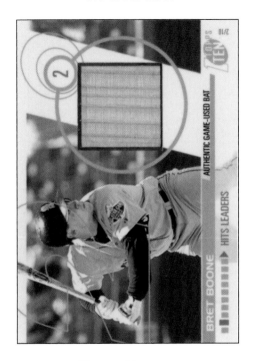

Bret Boone

2002 Topps Ten Bat Card

$5

Lou Boudreau
1951 Bowman
$40

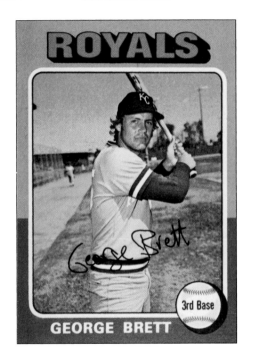

George Brett
1975 Topps Rookie Card
$45

George Brett
2004 Playoff Prime Cuts Material Signature
$150

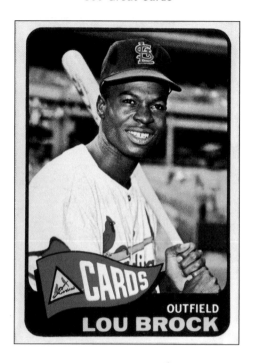

Lou Brock
1965 Topps
$28

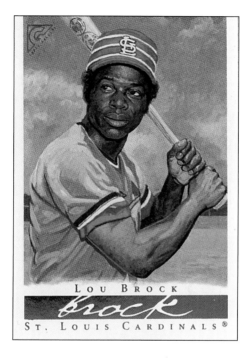

Lou Brock
2003 Topps Gallery Hall of Fame Edition
$1

Kevin Brown
2003 Leaf Certified Materials Mirror Blue
$8

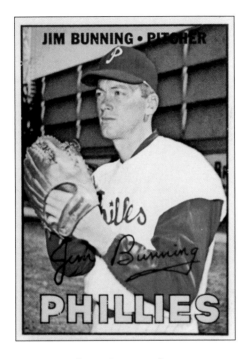

Jim Bunning
1967 Topps
$43

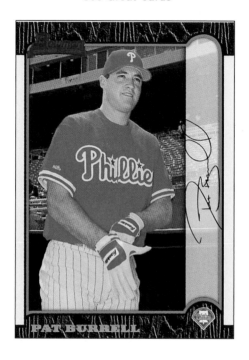

Pat Burrell
1999 Bowman Rookie Card
$4

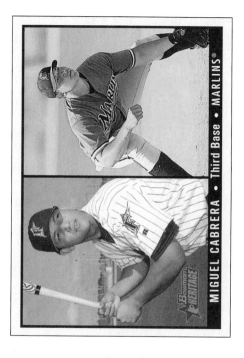

Miguel Cabrera
2003 Bowman Heritage
$1

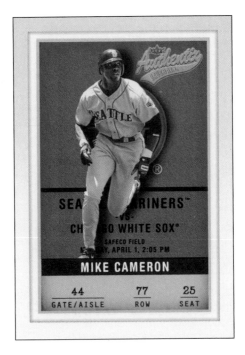

Mike Cameron
2002 Fleer Authentix
$1

Baseball Card Field Guide

Roy Campanella
1952 Topps
$1,700

Roy Campanella
1953 Topps
$200

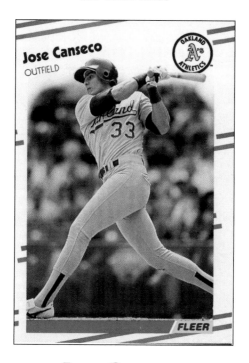

Jose Canseco
1988 Fleer
$1

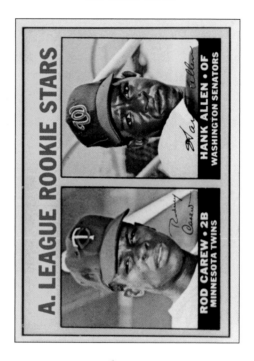

Rod Carew
1967 Topps Rookie Card
$120

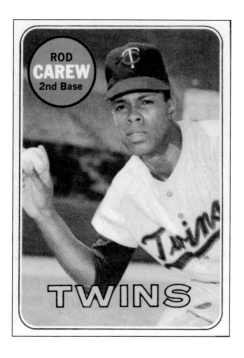

Rod Carew
1969 Topps
$18

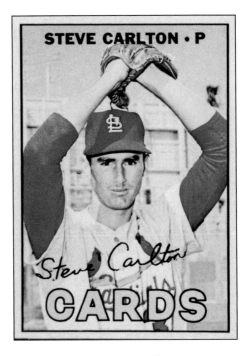

Steve Carlton
1967 Topps
$25

Joe Carter
1984 Donruss Rookie Card
$6

Joe Carter

2001 Donruss Rookie Reprint (replicates rookie card)

$3

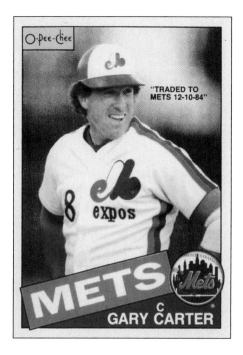

Gary Carter
1985 O-Pee-Chee
$2

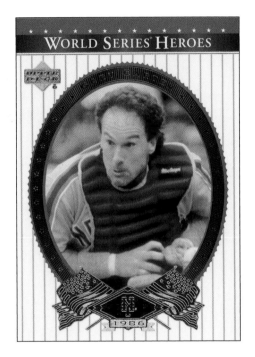

Gary Carter
2002 Upper Deck World Series Heroes
$1

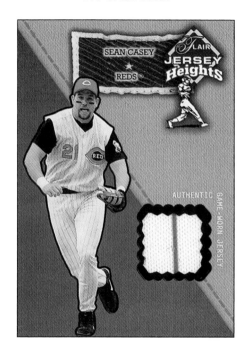

Sean Casey
2002 Fleer Flair Jersey Heights
$8

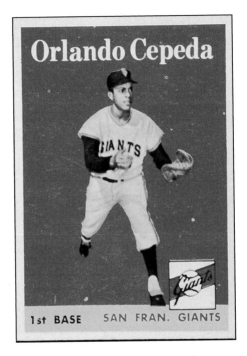

Orlando Cepeda

1st BASE   SAN FRAN. GIANTS

Orlando Cepeda
1958 Topps Rookie Card
$65

Orlando Cepeda
1959 Topps
$23

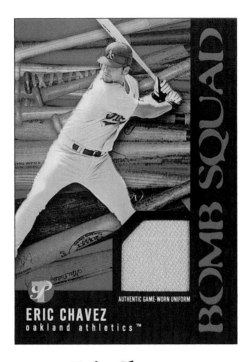

Eric Chavez

2003 Topps Pristine Bomb Squad Jersey Card

$4

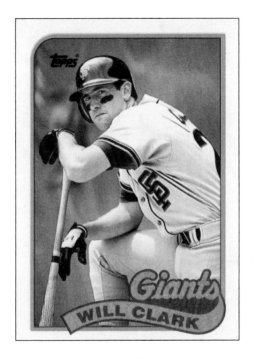

Will Clark
1989 Topps
$1

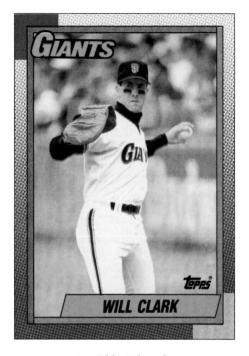

Will Clark

1990 Topps

$1

Baseball Card Field Guide

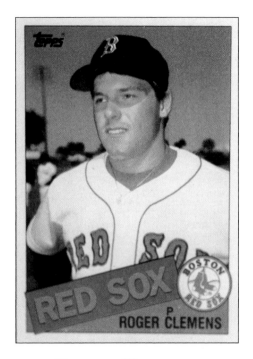

Roger Clemens
1985 Topps
$16

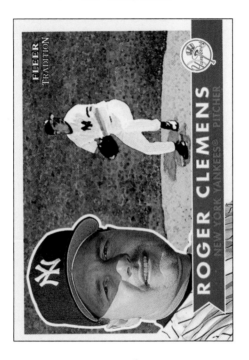

Roger Clemens
2001 Fleer Tradition
$2

BOB Clemente
PITTSBURGH PIRATES OUTFIELD

Roberto Clemente
1957 Topps
$160

BOB CLEMENTE
Outfield

Pittsburgh
Pirates

Roberto Clemente
1961 Topps
$90

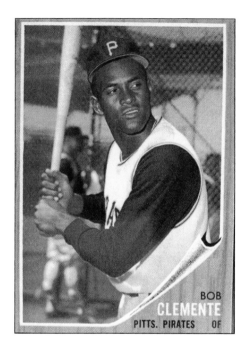

Roberto Clemente
1962 Topps
$90

COBB, DETROIT

Ty Cobb
1909-11 T206 White Borders, Green Background
$4,000

"TY" COBB

Ty Cobb
1911 Sporting Life Cabinet
$8,800

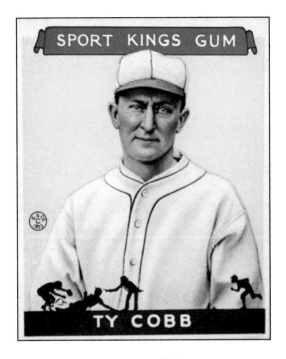

SPORT KINGS GUM

TY COBB

Ty Cobb
1933 Sport Kings
$3,000

Ty Cobb
1960 Fleer Baseball Greats
$34

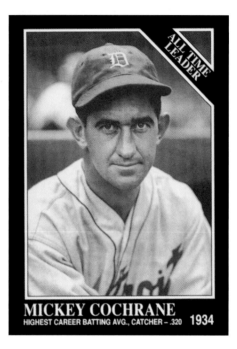

MICKEY COCHRANE
HIGHEST CAREER BATTING AVG., CATCHER – .320 1934

Mickey Cochrane
1991-95 Conlon Collection
$1

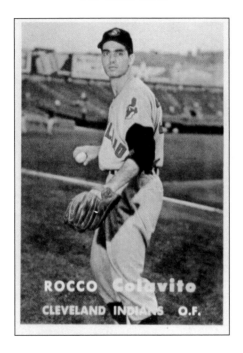

Rocky Colavito
1957 Topps Rookie Card
$95

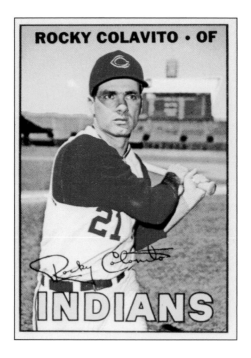

Rocky Colavito
1967 Topps
$75

David Cone
2001 Topps Heritage
$2

Johnny Damon
2003 Topps Gallery
$1

Andre Dawson
1993 Topps
$1

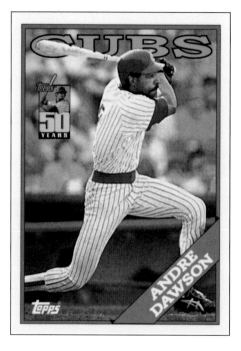

Andre Dawson
2001 Topps Chicago Cubs
$6

PLAYER PHOTO © 1934 BY H. A. MEADE
GRAND STAND PHOTO COURTESY ST. LOUIS POST-DISPATCH

Dizzy Dean
1935 Rice-Stix
$1,375

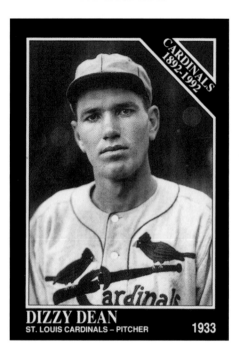

CARDINALS
1892-1992

DIZZY DEAN
ST. LOUIS CARDINALS – PITCHER

1933

Dizzy Dean
1991-95 Conlon Collection
$1

Carlos Delgado
1992 Bowman Rookie Card
$12

Carlos Delgado
2002 Topps206 Jersey Card
$8

BILL DICKEY

BIG LEAGUE CHEWING GUM

Bill Dickey
1933 Goudey
$625

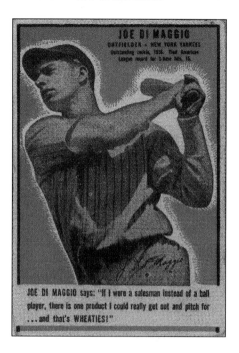

JOE DI MAGGIO
OUTFIELDER • NEW YORK YANKEES
Outstanding rookie, 1936. Tied American
League record for 1 base hits, 15.

JOE DI MAGGIO says: "If I were a salesman instead of a ball player, there is one product I could really get out and pitch for ...and that's WHEATIES!"

Joe DiMaggio
1937 Wheaties – Series 7
$300

"JOE" DI MAGGIO

Joe DiMaggio
1941 Play Ball
$2,450

Joe DiMaggio
1980-2001 Perez-Steele HOF Postcards
$35 (unsigned)

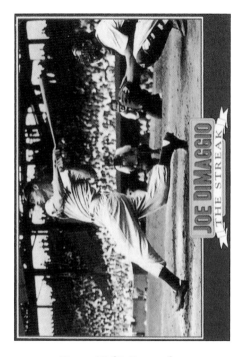

Joe DiMaggio
1992 Score Joe DiMaggio
$8

Larry Doby
1956 Topps
$40

J.D. Drew
2002 Donruss Diamond Kings Diamond Cut Collection
$40

DON DRYSDALE
Los Angeles Dodgers

Don Drysdale
1960 Post Cereal
$400

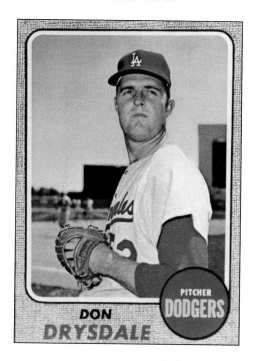

Don Drysdale
1968 Topps
$15

Adam Dunn
1999 Bowman Rookie Card
$6

Leo Durocher
1969 Topps
$5

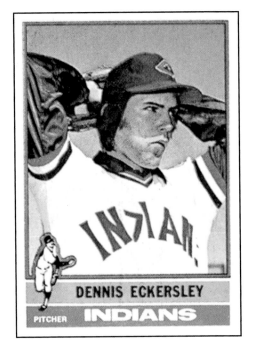

Dennis Eckersley
1976 Topps Rookie Card
$20

Dennis Eckersley

2002 Donruss Classics Significant Signatures

$20

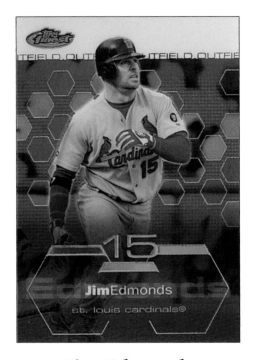

Jim Edmonds
2003 Topps Finest
$1

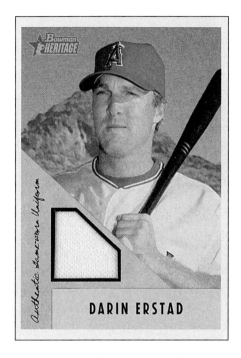

Darin Erstad
2002 Bowman Heritage Jersey Card
$6

Johnny Evers
1911 T3 Turkey Red Cabinets
$900

BOB FELLER
pitcher CLEVELAND INDIANS

Bob Feller
1953 Topps
$115

BOB FELLER
PITCHER
CLEVELAND INDIANS
Born: Van Meter, Iowa, Nov. 3, '18
Height: 6-1   Weight: 185
Bats: Right   Throws: Right
One of baseball's greatest pitchers, Bob, with the blazing fast ball, won 20 or more games for the sixth time in his career in the majors in 1951, winning 22 while losing only 8. Pitched a no-hitter in 1951, his third. Bob never played in the minors. He joined the Indians in 1936—and has been with them ever since, with the exception of three years spent in the service.

Bob Feller
1952 Red Man Tobacco
$70

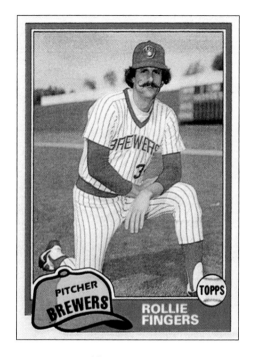

Rollie Fingers
1981 Topps Traded

$1

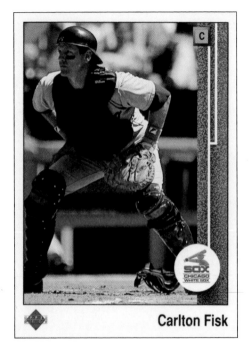

Carlton Fisk

Carlton Fisk
1989 Upper Deck
$1

Carlton Fisk
1993 Upper Deck
$1

Curt Flood
1967 Topps
$3

Whitey Ford
1957 Topps
$85

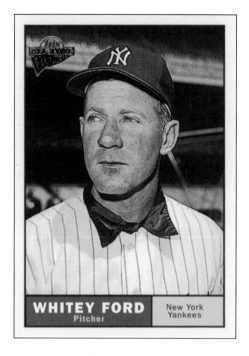

WHITEY FORD
Pitcher

New York
Yankees

Whitey Ford
2003 Topps All-Time Fan Favorites
$1

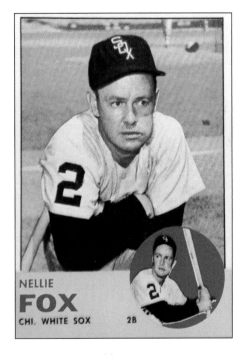

Nellie Fox
1963 Topps
$23

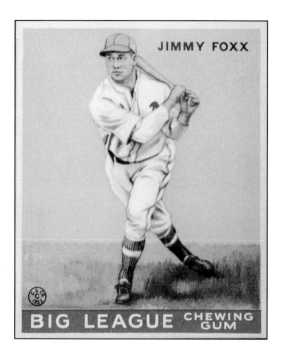

Jimmie Foxx
1933 Goudey
$1,165

Baseball Card Field Guide

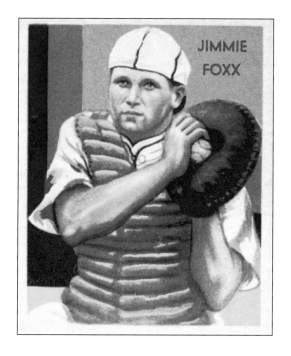

Jimmie Foxx
1934-36 Diamond Stars
$450

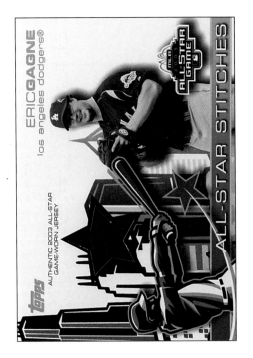

Eric Gagne

2004 Topps All Star Stitches

$8

Joe Garagiola
1953 Bowman Color
$40

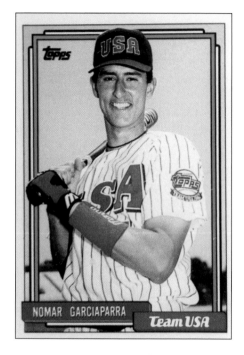

Nomar Garciaparra
1992 Topps Traded Rookie Card
$35

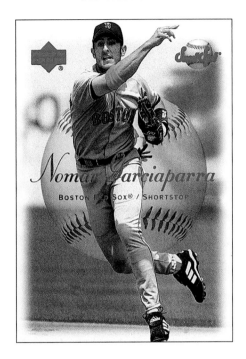

Nomar Garciaparra
2001 Upper Deck Sweet Spot
$2

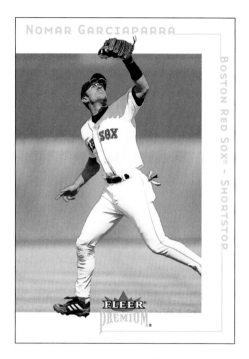

Nomar Garciaparra
2001 Fleer Premium
$2

Lou Gehrig
1933 Goudey
$5,500

Lou Gehrig
1948 Swell Sport Thrills
$185

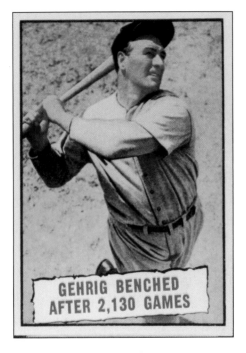

GEHRIG BENCHED
AFTER 2,130 GAMES

Lou Gehrig
1961 Topps
$35

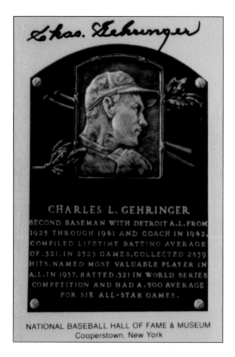

CHARLES L. GEHRINGER
SECOND BASEMAN WITH DETROIT A.L. FROM
1925 THROUGH 1941 AND COACH IN 1942.
COMPILED LIFETIME BATTING AVERAGE
OF .321 IN 2323 GAMES, COLLECTED 2839
HITS. NAMED MOST VALUABLE PLAYER IN
A.L. IN 1937. BATTED .321 IN WORLD SERIES
COMPETITION AND HAD A .500 AVERAGE
FOR SIX ALL-STAR GAMES.

NATIONAL BASEBALL HALL OF FAME & MUSEUM
Cooperstown, New York

Charlie Gehringer
1964-2003 HOF Yellow Plaque Postcards
$1 (unsigned)

Jason Giambi
1991 Topps Traded Rookie Card
$4

Jason Giambi • 1B —

OAKLAND ATHLETICS™

Jason Giambi
2001 Donruss Studio
$1

Jason Giambi
1998 Pacific Invincible

$2

Bob Gibson
1962 Topps
$80

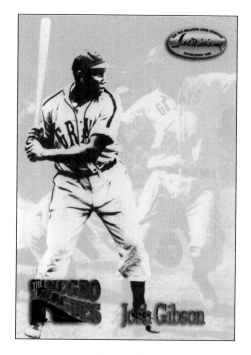

Josh Gibson
1993 Ted Williams Card. Co.
$1

BRIAN GILES / OF

Brian Giles
2002 Donruss Studio
$1

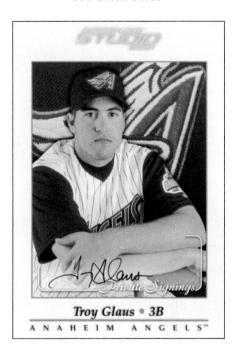

Troy Glaus
2001 Donruss Studio Private Signings
$20

Tom Glavine

1996 Upper Deck

$1

Baseball Card Field Guide

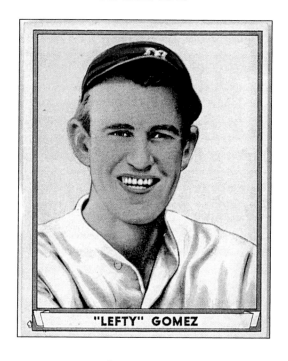

"LEFTY" GOMEZ

Lefty Gomez
1941 Play Ball
$450

Juan Gonzalez

1991 Fleer Ultra Update

$2

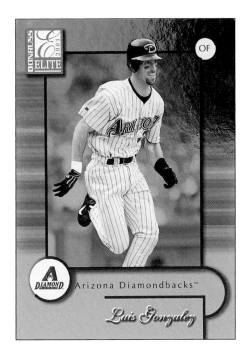

Luis Gonzalez
2001 Donruss Elite
$1

DWIGHT GOODEN *PREVIEW*
New York Mets

Dwight Gooden
1992 Studio Preview
$2

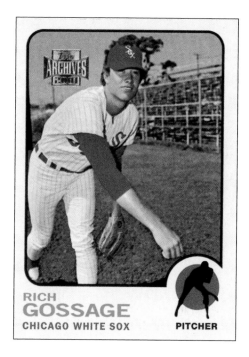

Goose Gossage
2001 Topps Archives (1973 Topps replica)
$1

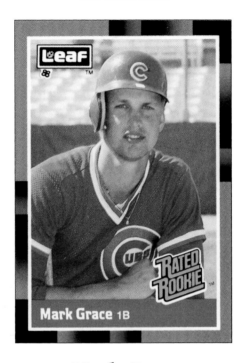

Mark Grace
1988 Leaf
$1

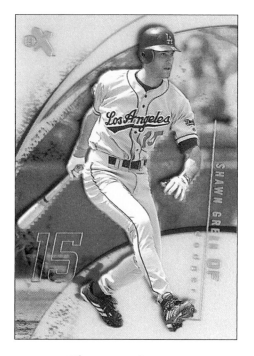

Shawn Green

2002 Fleer E-X

$1

Hank Greenberg

1934 Goudey

$725

Ken Griffey Jr.
1989 Upper Deck Rookie Card
$30

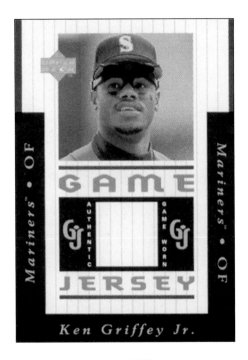

Ken Griffey Jr.
1997 Upper Deck Game Jersey
$150

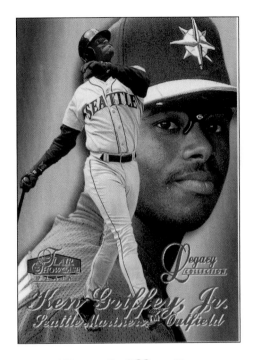

Ken Griffey Jr.
1997 Fleer Flair Showcase Legacy Collection
$40

Lefty Grove
1934 Goudey
$490

Vladimir Guerrero
1995 Bowman's Best Rookie Card
$70

Vladimir Guerrero
1995 Bowman Rookie Card
$50

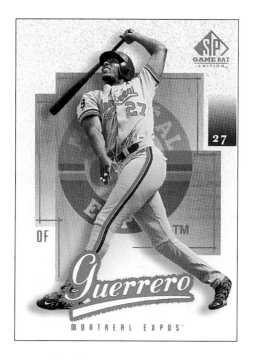

Vladimir Guerrero
2001 Upper Deck SP Game Bat Edition
$2

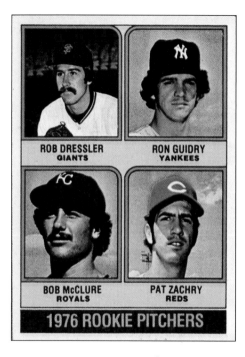

ROB DRESSLER
GIANTS

RON GUIDRY
YANKEES

BOB McCLURE
ROYALS

PAT ZACHRY
REDS

1976 ROOKIE PITCHERS

Ron Guidry
1976 Topps Rookie Card
$4

Tony Gwynn
1983 Topps Rookie Card
$15

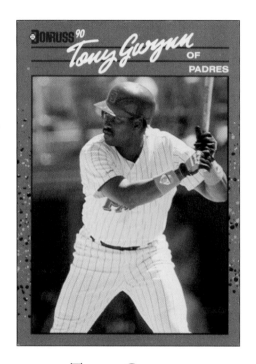

Tony Gwynn
1990 Donruss
$1

Tony Gwynn
2003 Playoff Piece of the Game Materials Jersey Card
$8

Roy Halladay

1997 Bowman Chrome Rookie Card

$12

Todd Helton
1993 Topps Traded Rookie Card
$10

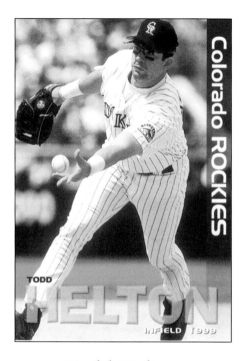

Todd Helton
1999 Colorado Rockies Police Set
$3

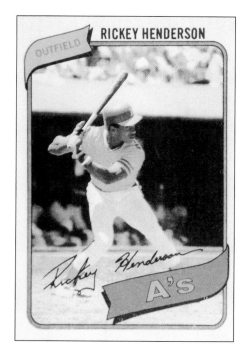

Rickey Henderson
1980 Topps Rookie Card
$19

Keith Hernandez

1985 Topps

$1

Baseball Card Field Guide

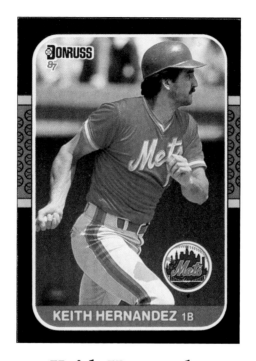

Keith Hernandez
1987 Donruss
$1

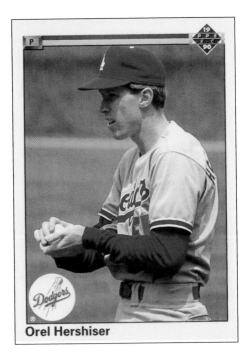

Orel Hershiser

Orel Hershiser
1990 Upper Deck
$1

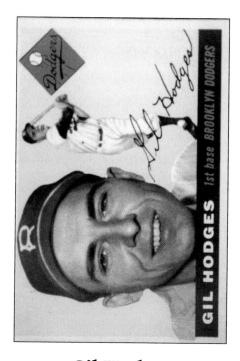

Gil Hodges
1955 Topps
$130

Trevor Hoffman

2002 San Diego Padres Keebler Set

$1

Rogers Hornsby

1934-36 Diamond Stars

$325

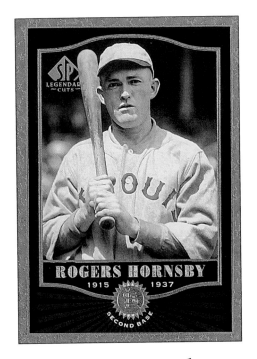

Rogers Hornsby
2001 SP Legendary Cuts
$1

Frank Howard
1964 Topps
$8

Elston Howard
1956 Topps
$50

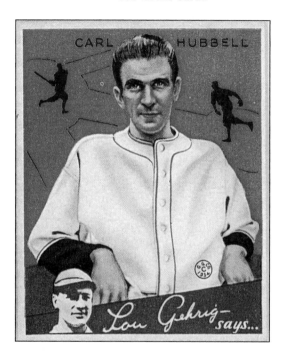

Carl Hubbell
1934 Goudey
$275

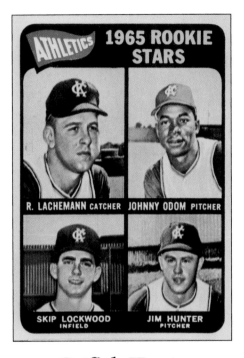

Catfish Hunter

1965 Topps Rookie Card

$45

Catfish Hunter
1968 Topps
$12

Monte Irvin
1954 Topps
$45

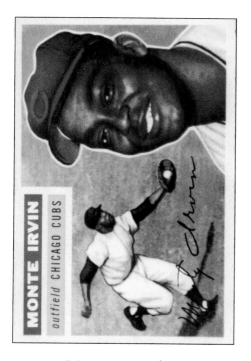

Monte Irvin
1956 Topps
$40

Bo Jackson
1992 Upper Deck
$1

JOE JACKSON
L. F.—Chicago White Sox
87

Joe Jackson
1916 The Sporting News
$4,000

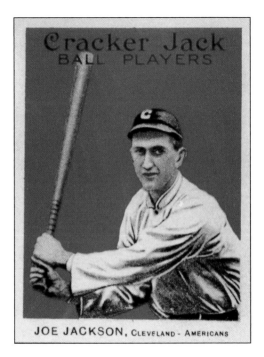

Joe Jackson
1915 Cracker Jack
$12,000

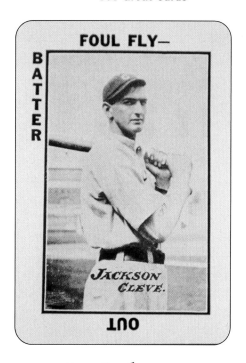

Joe Jackson
1913 National Game
$750

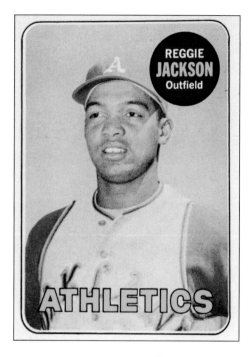

Reggie Jackson
1969 Topps Rookie Card
$135

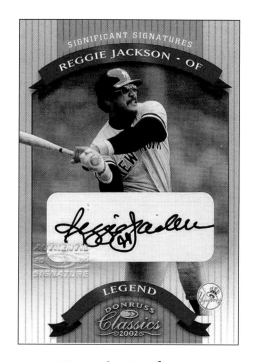

Reggie Jackson
2002 Donruss Classics Significant Signatures
$40

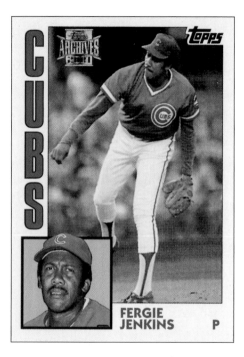

Ferguson Jenkins
2001 Topps Archives (1984 Topps replica)
$1

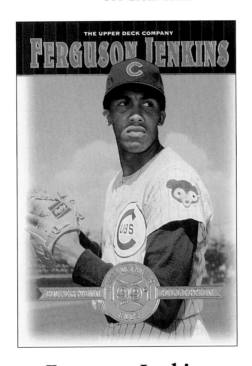

Ferguson Jenkins
2001 Upper Deck Hall of Famers
$1

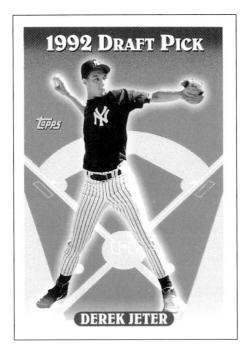

Derek Jeter
1993 Topps Rookie Card
$3

Derek Jeter
1993 Bowman Rookie Card
$12

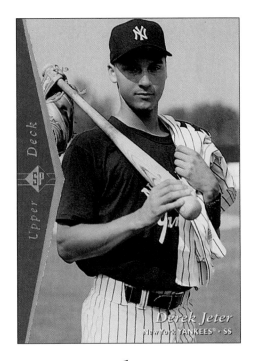

Derek Jeter
1995 Upper Deck SP
$2

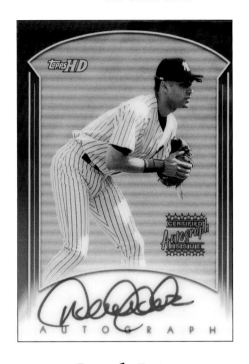

Derek Jeter

2000 Topps HD Autograph

$150

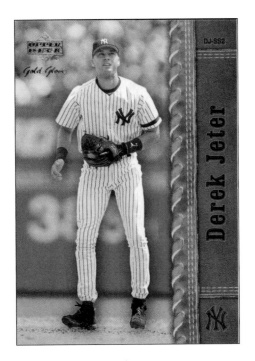

Derek Jeter
2001 Upper Deck Gold Glove

$4

TOMMY JOHN • PITCHER

WHITE SOX

Tommy John
1967 Topps
$60

Randy Johnson
2002 Donruss Diamond Kings Diamond Cut Collection
$15

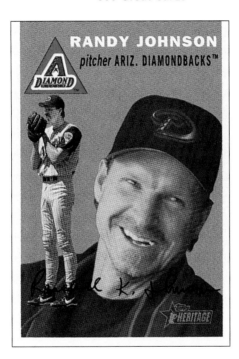

Randy Johnson
2003 Topps Heritage
$2

JOHNSON
Pitcher, Washington A. L.

Walter Johnson
1909 Ramly Cigarettes
$9,000

JOHNSON, WASHINGTON

Walter Johnson
1909-11 T206 White Borders
$1,775

JOHNSON WASHINGTON

Walter Johnson
1911 Turkey Red Cabinets
$3,000

JOHNSON, WASHINGTON - AMERICANS

Walter Johnson
1915 Cracker Jack
$4,750

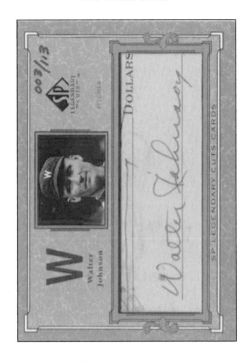

Walter Johnson
2001 Upper Deck SP Legendary Cuts Signatures
$510

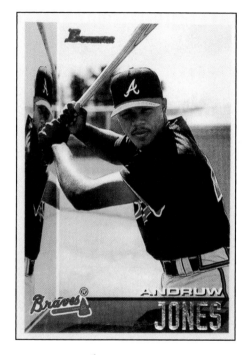

Andruw Jones
1995 Bowman Rookie Card
$25

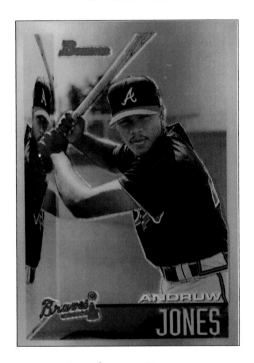

Andruw Jones

2002 Bowman Chrome Rookie Reprint

$2

Chipper Jones
2002 Bowman Heritage
$2

CHIPPER JONES / OF

Chipper Jones
2002 Donruss Studio
$2

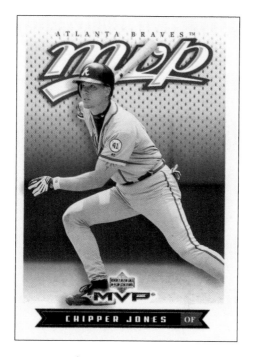

Chipper Jones
2003 Upper Deck MVP
$1

Jim Kaat
1982 Donruss
$1

Al Kaline
1956 Topps
$75

Al Kaline
1964 Topps
$24

Austin Kearns
1999 Bowman Chrome Rookie Card
$25

KEELER N.Y. NATL

Willie Keeler
1911 Turkey Red Cabinets
$900

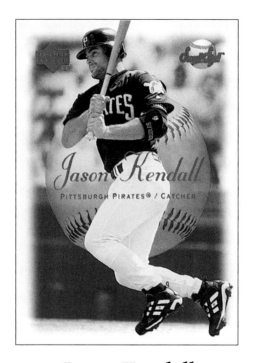

Jason Kendall
2001 Upper Deck Sweet Spot
$1

Jeff Kent
2000 Fleer Showcase

$1

Baseball Card Field Guide

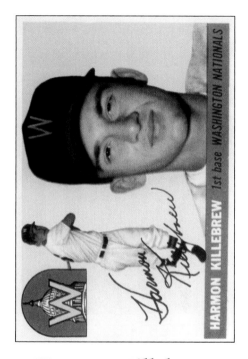

Harmon Killebrew
1955 Topps Rookie Card
$175

Harmon Killebrew

1960 Post Cereal

$400

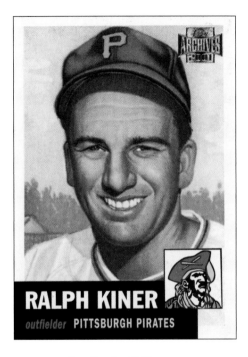

Ralph Kiner

2001 Topps Archives (1953 Topps replica)

$1

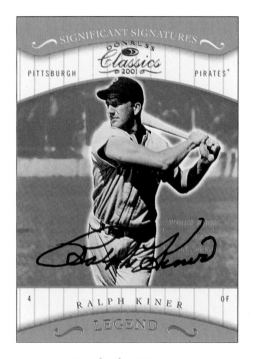

Ralph Kiner
2001 Donruss Classics Significant Signatures
$25

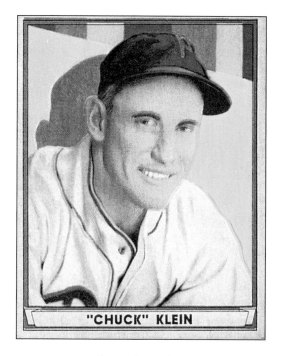

"CHUCK" KLEIN

Chuck Klein
1941 Play Ball
$215

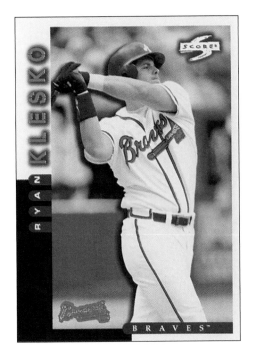

Ryan Klesko
1998 Score Team Collection
$1

Baseball Card Field Guide

Ted Kluszewski
1953 Bowman Color
$75

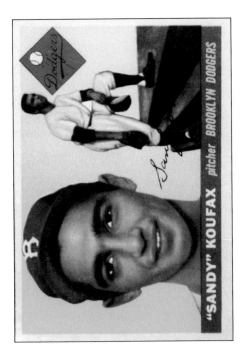

Sandy Koufax
1955 Topps Rookie Card
$465

Sandy Koufax
1959 Topps
$100

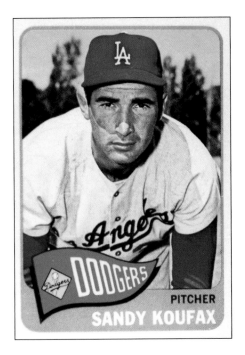

Sandy Koufax
1965 Topps
$85

Tony Kubek
1958 Topps
$25

HARVEY KUENN

DETROIT TIGERS

Harvey Kuenn
1954 Red Heart Dog Food
$45

Lajoie—Cleveland Am.

Nap Lajoie
1911 Mecca Double Folders
$200

LAJOIE, CLEVELAND

Nap Lajoie
1909-11 T206 White Borders
$600

Nap Lajoie
1933 Goudey (issued in 1934)
$23,000

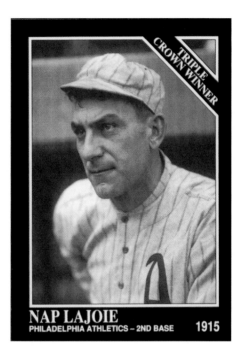

NAP LAJOIE
PHILADELPHIA ATHLETICS – 2ND BASE   1915

Nap Lajoie
1991-95 Conlon Collection
$1

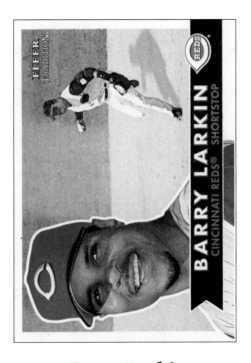

Barry Larkin

2001 Fleer Tradition

$1

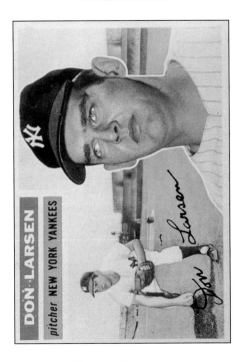

Don Larsen
1956 Topps
$65

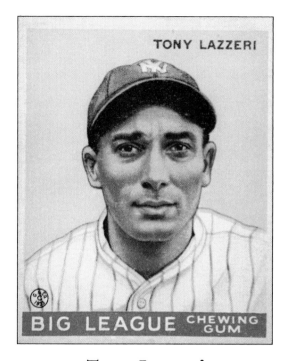

Tony Lazzeri
1933 Goudey
$500

BUCK LEONARD

Buck Leonard
1990 Stars of the Negro Leagues
$1

Baseball Card Field Guide

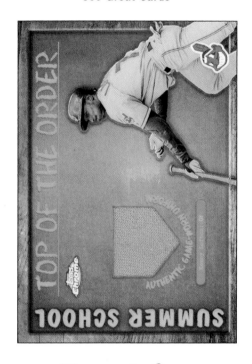

Kenny Lofton
2002 Topps Chrome Summer School Jersey Card
$5

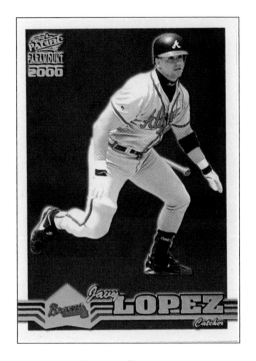

Javy Lopez

2000 Pacific Paramount

$1

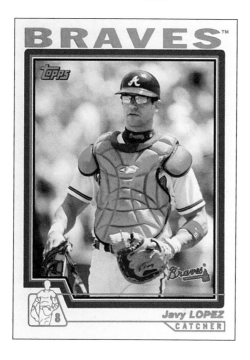

Javy Lopez
2004 Topps
$1

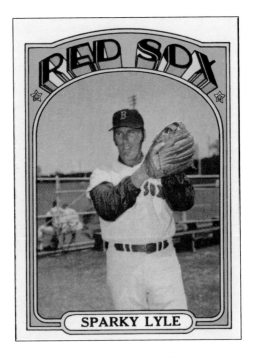

Sparky Lyle
1972 Topps
$2

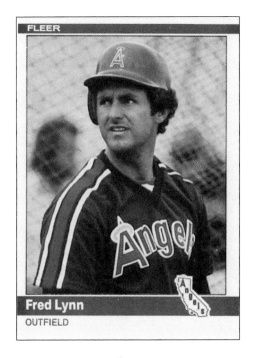

FLEER

Fred Lynn
OUTFIELD

Fred Lynn
1984 Fleer
$1

PHILADELPHIA ATHLETICS   **MANAGER**

Connie Mack
1998 Philadelphia Fan Favorites
$1

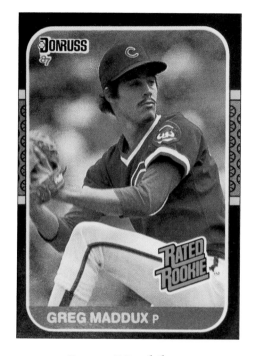

Greg Maddux
1987 Donruss Rookie Card
$5

Greg Maddux
1989 Bowman
$1

Mickey Mantle
1952 Topps
$11,000

Mickey Mantle
1956 Topps
$840

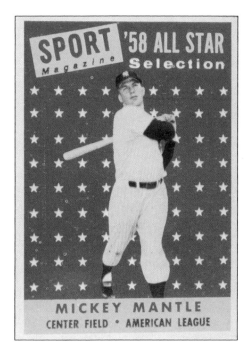

Mickey Mantle
1958 Topps All-Star
$100

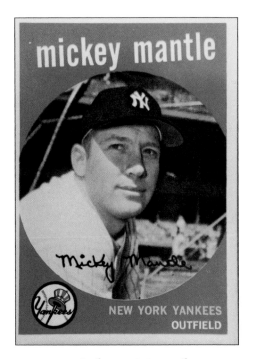

mickey mantle

NEW YORK YANKEES
OUTFIELD

Mickey Mantle
1959 Topps
$475

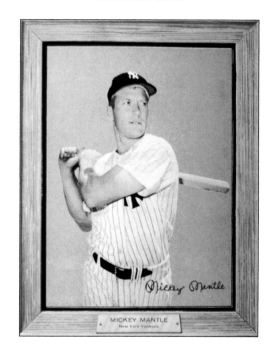

Mickey Mantle
1960 Post Cereal
$1,800

MICKEY MANTLE
Outfield

New York
Yankees

Mickey Mantle
1961 Topps
$260

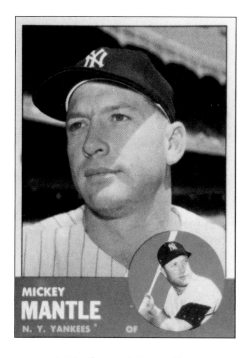

Mickey Mantle
1963 Topps
$310

Mickey Mantle
2000 Fleer Tradition Update Mantle Pieces Jersey Card
$150

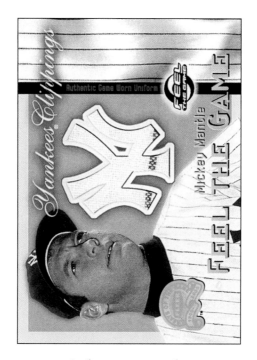

Mickey Mantle

2000 Fleer Greats of the Game Yankees Clippings Jersey Card

$260

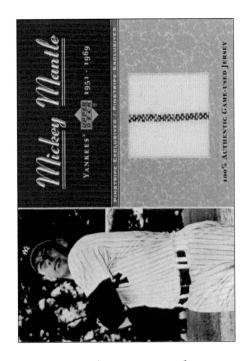

Mickey Mantle

2001 Upper Deck MVP Mantle Pinstripes Memorabilia

$125

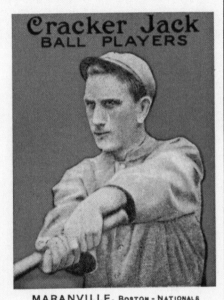

Cracker Jack
BALL PLAYERS

MARANVILLE, BOSTON - NATIONALS

Rabbit Maranville
1914 Cracker Jack reprint card
$1

Rabbit Maranville
1960 Fleer Baseball Greats
$5

Juan Marichal
1964 Topps
$13

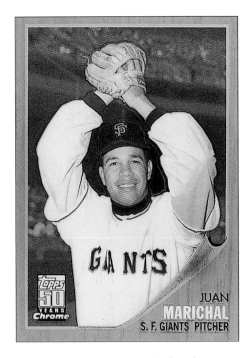

Juan Marichal
2001 Topps Chrome Through the Years
$2

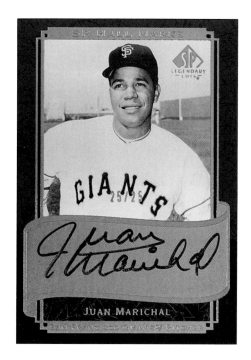

Juan Marichal
2003 Upper Deck SP Legendary Cuts Hall Marks
$35

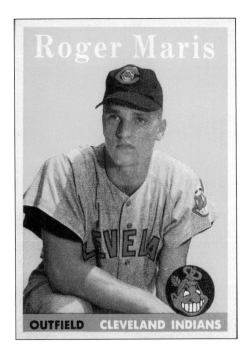

Roger Maris
1958 Topps Rookie Card
$290

Roger Maris
1959 Topps
$75

Roger Maris
1962 Topps
$235

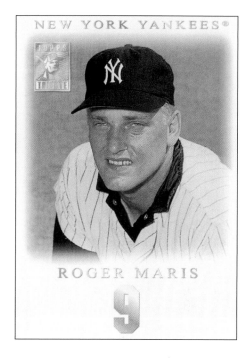

Roger Maris
2001 Topps Tribute
$10

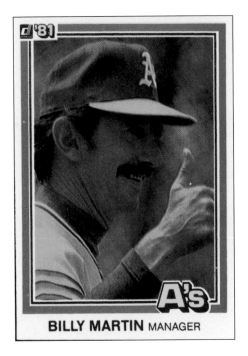

BILLY MARTIN MANAGER

Billy Martin
1981 Donruss
$1

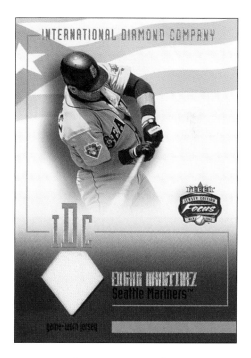

Edgar Martinez

2002 Fleer Focus Jersey Edition International Diamond Co.

$5

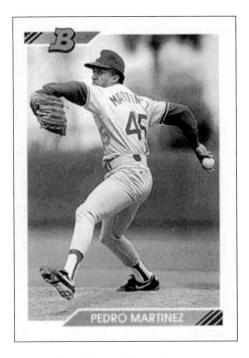

Pedro Martinez

1992 Bowman

$5

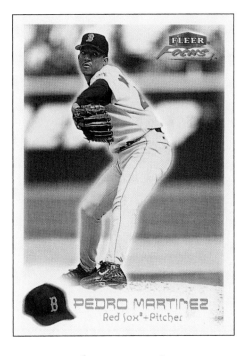

Pedro Martinez

2000 Fleer Focus

$1

Pedro Martinez

2001 Donruss Elite

$4

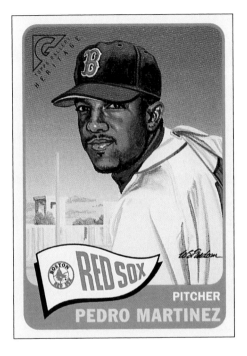

Pedro Martinez
2001 Topps Gallery Heritage
$3

Eddie Mathews
1954 Bowman
$60

Eddie Mathews
1963 Topps
$18

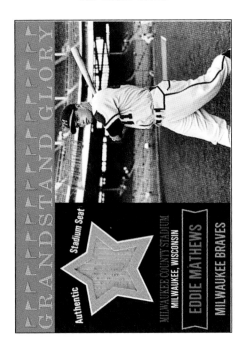

Eddie Mathews

2003 Topps Heritage Grandstand Glory

$12

MATHEWSON, N. Y. NAT'L

Christy Mathewson
1909-11 T206 White Borders
$1,325

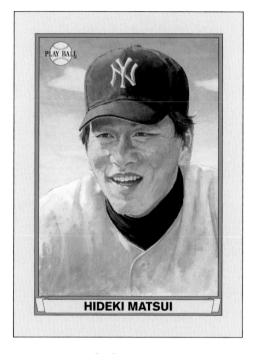

HIDEKI MATSUI

Hideki Matsui

2003 Upper Deck Play Ball Rookie Card

$8

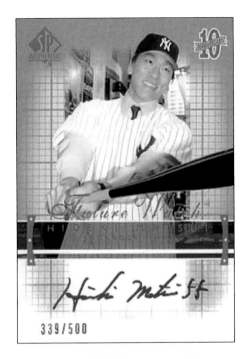

339/500

Hideki Matsui
2003 Upper Deck SP Authentic Rookie Card
$375

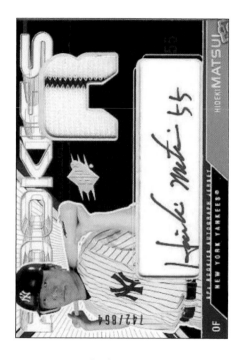

Hideki Matsui
2003 Upper Deck SP^X Rookie Card
$250

Don Mattingly
1984 Donruss Rookie Card
$25

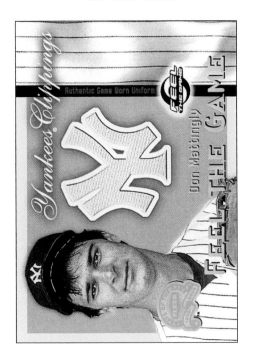

Don Mattingly

2000 Fleer Greats of the Game Yankees Clippings Jersey Card

$100

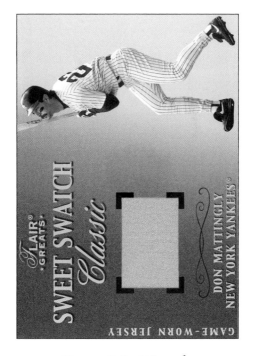

Don Mattingly

2003 Fleer Flair Greats Sweet Swatch Heroes Jersey Card

$35

Joe Mauer
2002 Bowman Rookie Card
$8

Willie Mays
1954 Topps
$355

Willie Mays

1958 Topps

$195

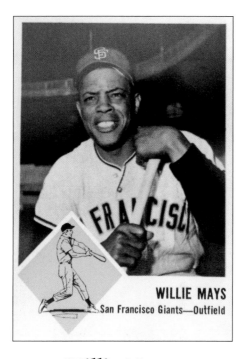

WILLIE MAYS
San Francisco Giants—Outfield

Willie Mays
1963 Fleer
$95

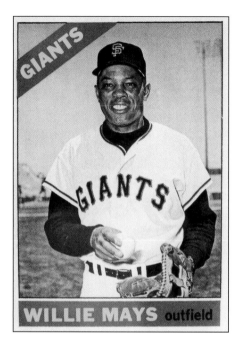

Willie Mays
1966 Topps
$145

Bill Mazeroski
1963 Fleer
$25

Bill Mazeroski
1964 Topps
$30

Tim McCarver
1964 Topps
$8

Willie McCovey

1962 Topps

$70

John McGraw
1911 T3 Turkey Red Cabinets
$900

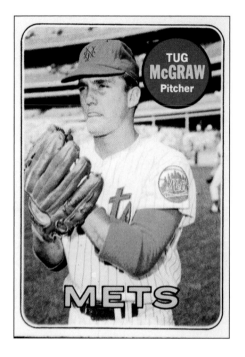

Tug McGraw
1969 Topps
$3

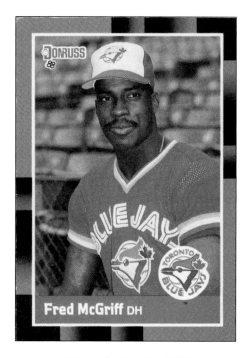

Fred McGriff

1988 Donruss

$1

Mark McGwire

1985 Topps Rookie Card

$30

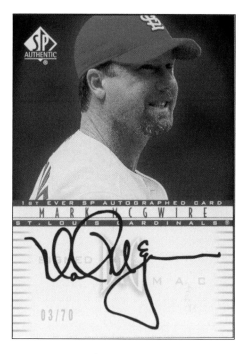

Mark McGwire
2002 Upper Deck SP Authentic Chirography
$500

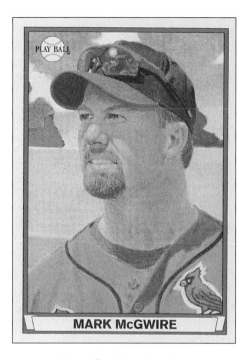

MARK McGWIRE

Mark McGwire
2003 Upper Deck Play Ball
$3

Kevin Millwood
2003 Fleer Genuine
$1

Minnie Minoso
1954 Bowman
$28

Baseball Card Field Guide

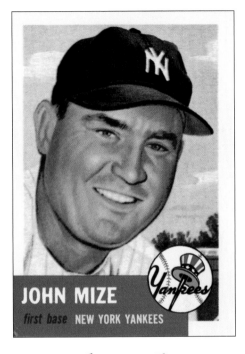

JOHN MIZE
first base NEW YORK YANKEES

Johnny Mize
1953 Topps
$85

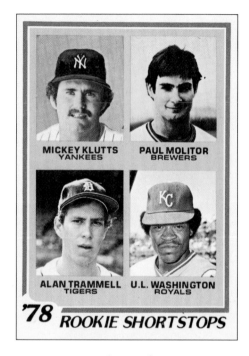

MICKEY KLUTTS
YANKEES

PAUL MOLITOR
BREWERS

ALAN TRAMMELL
TIGERS

U.L. WASHINGTON
ROYALS

'78 ROOKIE SHORTSTOPS

Paul Molitor
1978 Topps Rookie Card
$18

Paul Molitor
1981 Topps
$2

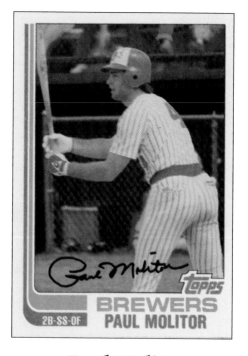

Paul Molitor
1982 Topps
$2

Paul Molitor

2001 Donruss Diamond Kings Reprint

$8

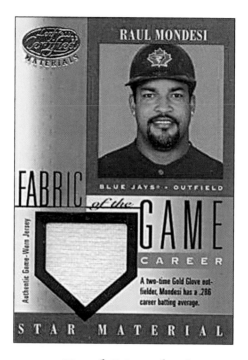

Raul Mondesi

2001 Leaf Certified Materials Fabric of the Game Jersey Card

$5

Joe Morgan
1965 Topps Rookie Card
$45

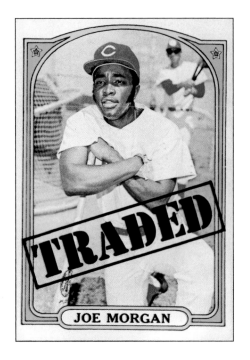

JOE MORGAN

Joe Morgan
1972 Topps
$23

Mark Mulder
2002 Leaf Clubhouse Signatures
$20

Thurman Munson   New York Yankees

Thurman Munson
1975 SSPC Puzzle Backs
$2

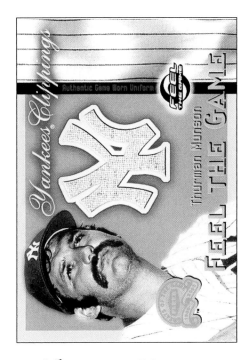

Thurman Munson

2000 Fleer Greats of the Game Yankees Clippings Jersey Card

$80

Thurman Munson

2002 Upper Deck SP Legendary Cuts

$1

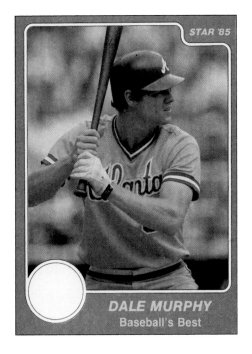

Dale Murphy
1986 Star '86
$5

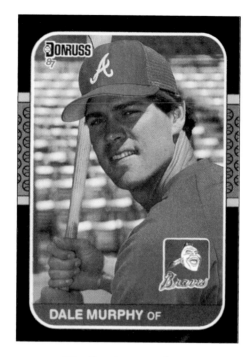

DALE MURPHY OF

Dale Murphy
1987 Donruss
$1

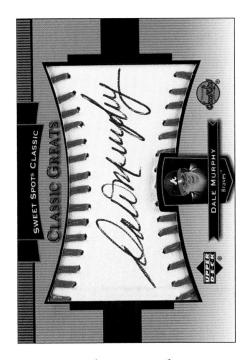

Dale Murphy
2003 Upper Deck Sweet Spot Classic Autograph
$30

Eddie Murray
1978 Topps Rookie Card
$18

Eddie Murray
1994 Donruss Triple Play
$1

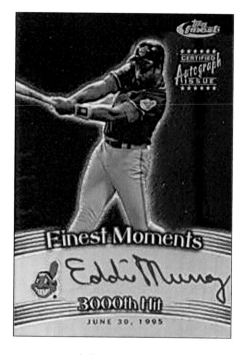

Eddie Murray
2001 Finest Moments Autograph
$20

Stan Musial
1953 Bowman Color
$485

Stan Musial
1959 Topps
$90

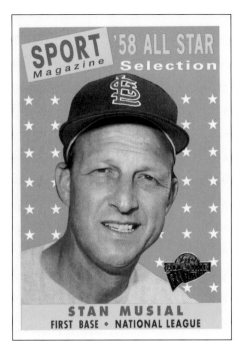

Stan Musial

2003 Topps All-Time Fan Favorites

$3

Mike Mussina

1999 Topps Stadium Club

$1

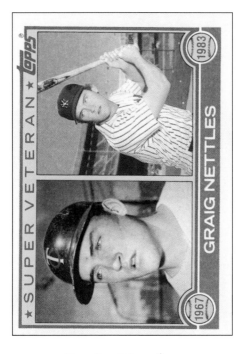

Graig Nettles
1983 Topps

$1

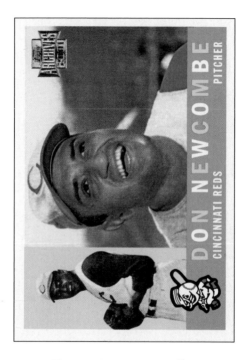

Don Newcombe

2001 Topps Archives (1960 Topps replica)

$1

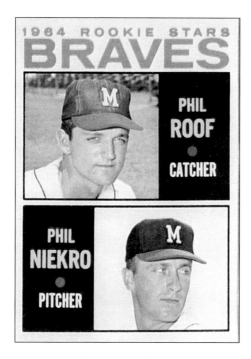

Phil Niekro
1964 Topps Rookie Card
$50

Hideo Nomo
1991 Calbee (Japanese)
$20

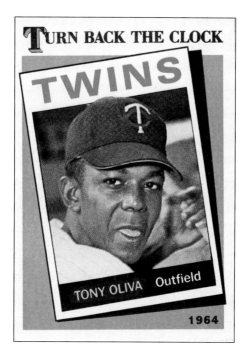

Tony Oliva
1989 Topps
$1

Magglio Ordonez
1998 Bowman Rookie Card
$4

Magglio Ordonez
2002 Topps Reserve Game Worn Uniform
$6

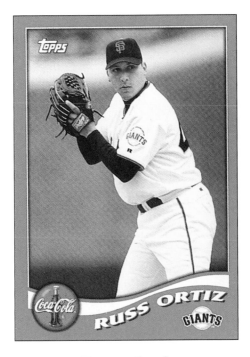

Russ Ortiz

2002 San Francisco Giants Coca-Cola

$1

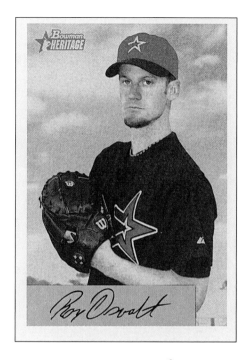

Roy Oswalt
2002 Bowman Heritage
$1

MEL OTT

Mel Ott
1960 Fleer Baseball Greats
$5

Satchel Paige
1953 Topps
$495

Satchel Paige
1980-2001 Perez-Steele HOF Postcards
$25 (unsigned)

SATCHEL PAIGE

Satchel Paige
1990 Eclipse Stars of the Negro Leagues
$2

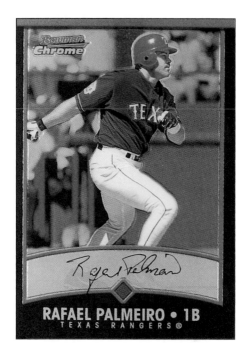

Rafael Palmeiro

2001 Bowman Chrome

$1

Rafael Palmeiro

2003 Topps205 Relics Jersey Card

$5

JIM PALMER — pitcher

Jim Palmer
1966 Topps Rookie Card
$50

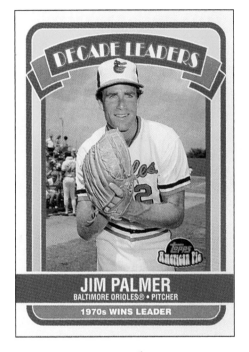

Jim Palmer
2001 Topps American Pie Decade Leaders
$1

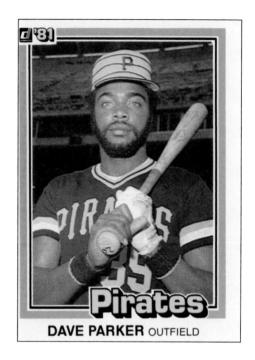

DAVE PARKER OUTFIELD

Dave Parker
1981 Donruss
$1

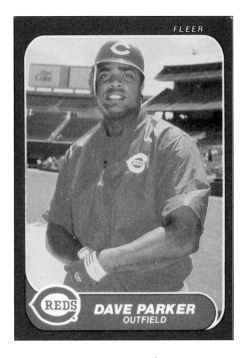

Dave Parker
1986 Fleer
$1

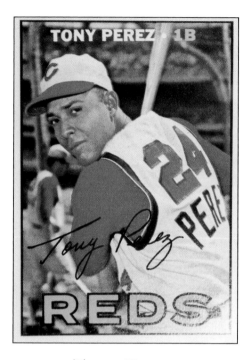

Tony Perez
1967 Topps
$38

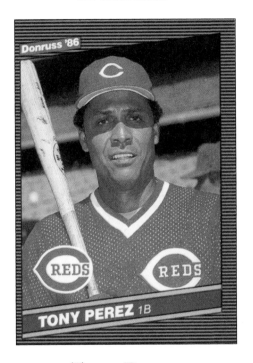

Tony Perez

1986 Donruss

$1

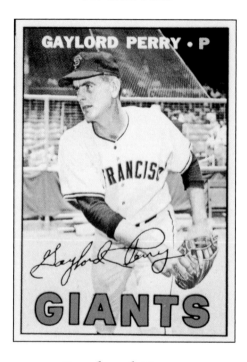

Gaylord Perry
1967 Topps
$14

Gaylord Perry
1981 Donruss
$2

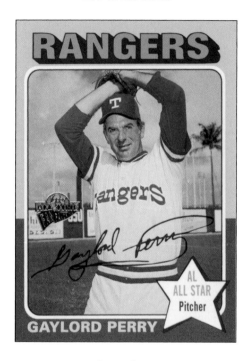

Gaylord Perry
2003 Topps All-Time Fan Favorites
$1

Andy Pettitte

2003 Leaf Certified Materials Fabric of the Game Jersey Card

$6

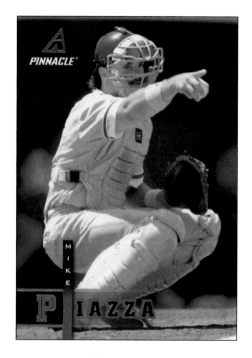

Mike Piazza
1998 Pinnacle Plus
$2

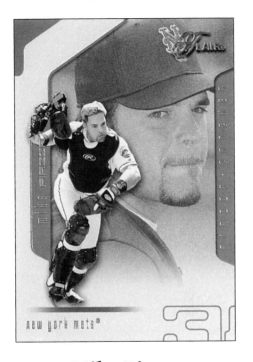

Mike Piazza
2002 Fleer Flair

$2

Mike Piazza
2000 Topps Subway Series Fan Fare (Subway Token)
$120

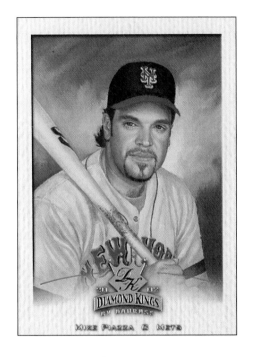

Mike Piazza

2002 Donruss Diamond Kings

$3

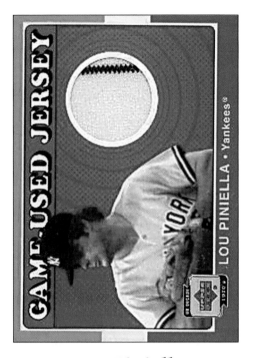

Lou Piniella

2001 Upper Deck Decade Game Jersey

$10

PLANK, PHILA. AMER.

Eddie Plank
1909-11 T206 White Borders
$60,000

Boog Powell
1962 Topps Rookie Card
$20

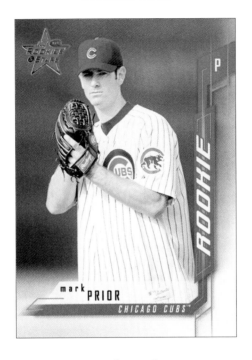

Mark Prior

2001 Leaf Rookies & Stars Rookie Card

$75

Mark Prior

2001 Donruss Elite Rookie Card

$140

Mark Prior
2001 Leaf Limited Autographed Rookie Card
$165

Mark Prior

2003 Upper Deck Standing O Die Cut Disc

$1

Kirby Puckett
1985 Donruss
$8

KIRBY PUCKETT *CF*
Minnesota Twins

Kirby Puckett
1992 Studio
$1

Minnesota Twins®

Kirby Puckett
2002 Fleer Greats of the Game
$3

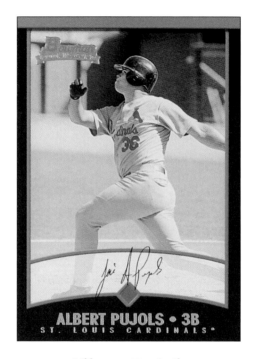

Albert Pujols

2001 Bowman Rookie Card

$20

Albert Pujols
2001 Donruss Elite Rookie Card
$160

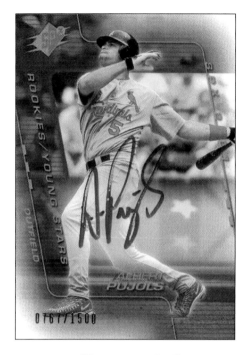

Albert Pujols
2001 Upper Deck Rookie Update SP^X Autographed Rookie Card
$300

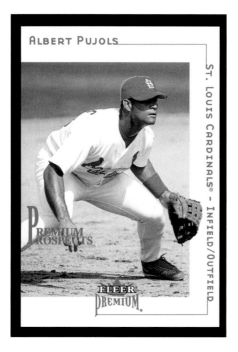

Albert Pujols
2001 Fleer Premium Rookie Card
$60

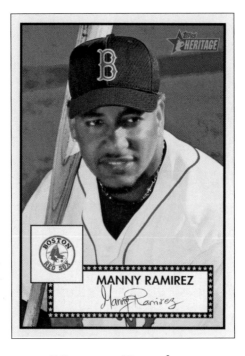

Manny Ramirez
2001 Topps Heritage
$1

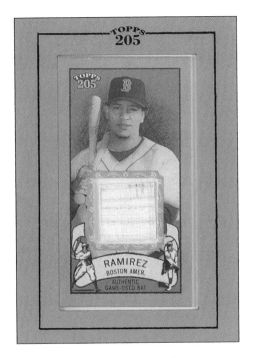

Manny Ramirez
2003 Topps205 Relic
$8

Pee Wee Reese
1947 Bond Bread
$100

Baseball Card Field Guide

Pee Wee Reese

1956 Topps

$110

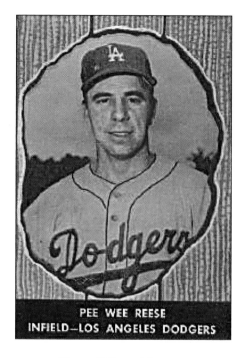

PEE WEE REESE
INFIELD—LOS ANGELES DODGERS

Pee Wee Reese
1958 Hires Root Beer
$100

Jim Rice
1983 Topps
$1

Jim Rice
2001 Fleer Red Sox 100th Anniversary Red Sox Threads
$20

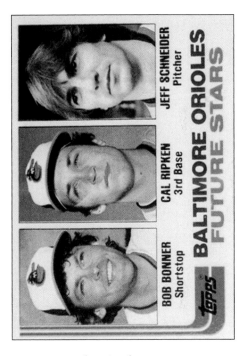

Cal Ripken Jr.
1982 Topps Rookie Card
$30

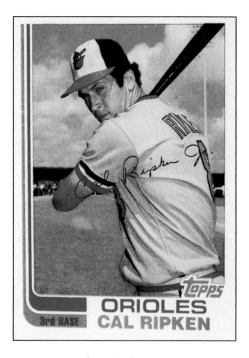

Cal Ripken Jr.
1982 Topps Traded
$110

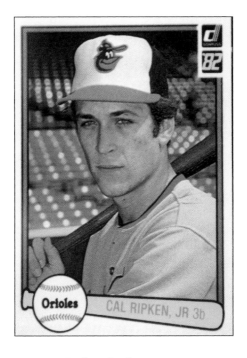

Cal Ripken Jr.
1982 Donruss Rookie Card
$20

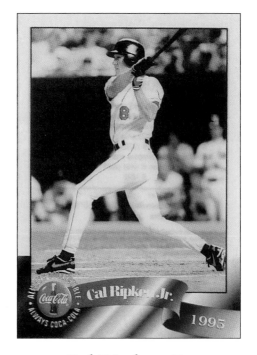

Cal Ripken Jr.

1996 Coca-Cola Cal Ripken Phone Card Cel

$1

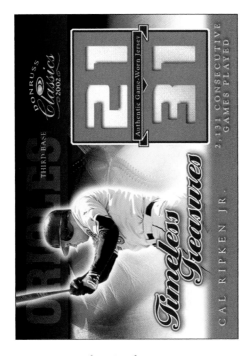

Cal Ripken Jr.
2002 Donruss Classics Timeless Treasures Jersey Card
$100

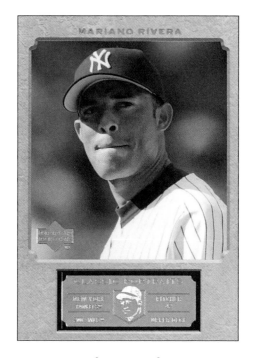

Mariano Rivera
2003 Upper Deck Classic Portraits
$1

Mariano Rivera
2003 Fleer Tradition
$1

Phil Rizzuto
1954 Topps
$90

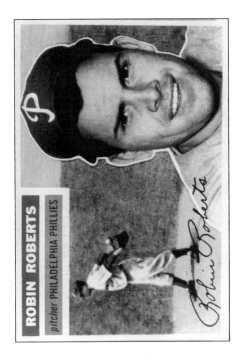

Robin Roberts
1956 Topps
$45

Robin Roberts

PITCHER PHILADELPHIA PHILS.

Robin Roberts
1958 Topps
$25

BROOKS Robinson
BALTIMORE ORIOLES 3rd B.

Brooks Robinson
1957 Topps Rookie Card
$230

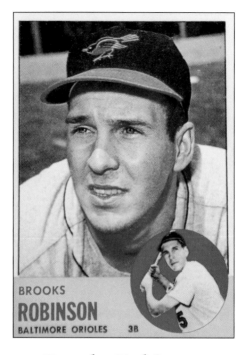

BROOKS
ROBINSON
BALTIMORE ORIOLES   3B

Brooks Robinson
1963 Topps
$40

BROOKS ROBINSON • 3B

ORIOLES

Brooks Robinson
1967 Topps
$150

Frank Robinson
1958 Topps
$55

Frank Robinson
1963 Topps
$30

Frank Robinson

1964 Topps

$23

Jackie Robinson
1953 Topps
$675

Jackie Robinson
1954 Topps
$200

Jackie Robinson
1955 Topps
$220

Jackie Robinson
1956 Topps
$145

Alex Rodriguez
1994 Upper Deck SP Rookie Card
$65

Alex Rodriguez
2002 Donruss Diamond Kings Studio
$8

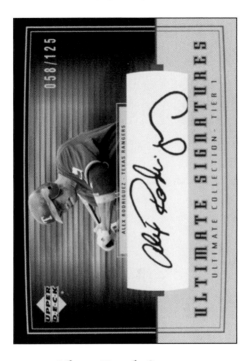

Alex Rodriguez
2002 Upper Deck Ultimate Collection Signatures Tier 1
$100

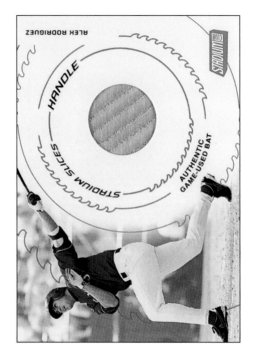

Alex Rodriguez
2003 Topps Stadium Club Stadium Slices Handle
$15

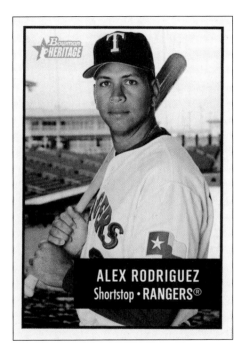

Alex Rodriguez
2004 Bowman Heritage
$1

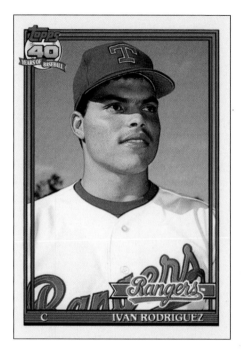

Ivan Rodriguez
1991 Topps Traded Rookie Card
$2

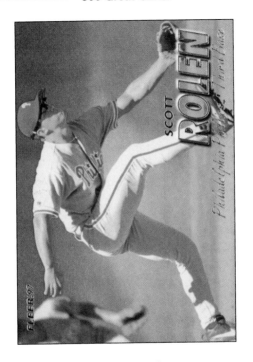

Scott Rolen
1997 Fleer
$1

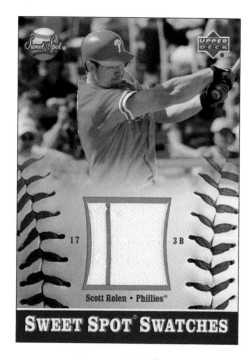

Scott Rolen

2002 Upper Deck Sweet Spot Sweet Swatches

$6

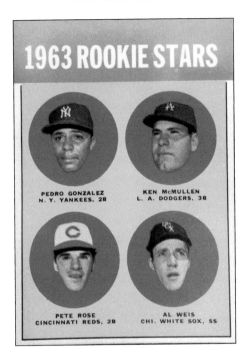

1963 ROOKIE STARS

PEDRO GONZALEZ
N. Y. YANKEES, 2B

KEN McMULLEN
L. A. DODGERS, 3B

PETE ROSE
CINCINNATI REDS, 2B

AL WEIS
CHI. WHITE SOX, SS

Pete Rose
1963 Topps Rookie Card
$525

REDS

PETE ROSE   2nd base

TOPPS 1963
ALL-STAR
ROOKIE

Pete Rose
1964 Topps
$135

Pete Rose
1965 Topps
$95

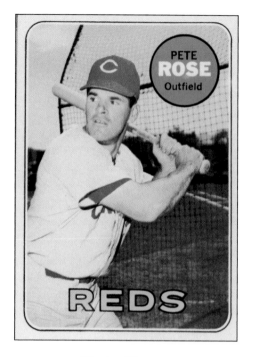

PETE
ROSE
Outfield

Pete Rose
1969 Topps
$28

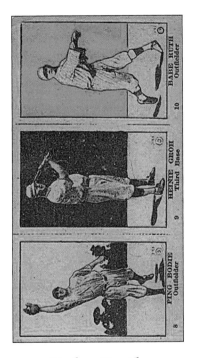

Babe Ruth
1921 Strip Card
$935

Babe Ruth
1932 Sanella Margarine (German)
$500

Babe Ruth
1933 Goudey No. 181
$5,300

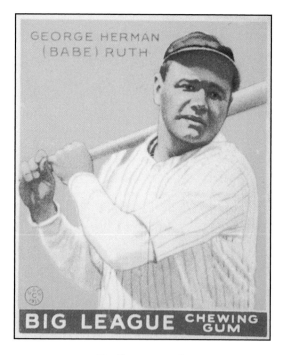

Babe Ruth
1933 Goudey No. 53
$7,500

Babe Ruth
1980-2001 Perez-Steele HOF Postcards
$45

Babe Ruth

2001 Upper Deck Sweet Spot Classics Bat Barrel

$700

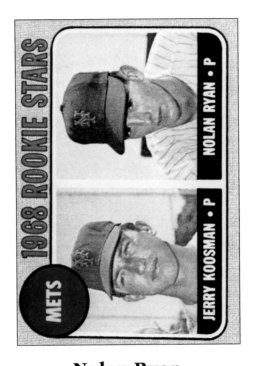

Nolan Ryan
1968 Topps Rookie Card
$315

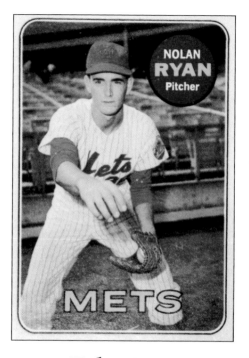

Nolan Ryan
1969 Topps
$113

Nolan Ryan
1970 Topps
$105

Nolan Ryan
1972 Topps
$58

Nolan Ryan

1982 Donruss Diamond Kings

$2

Nolan Ryan
2002 Upper Deck Sweet Spot Classic Signatures
$300

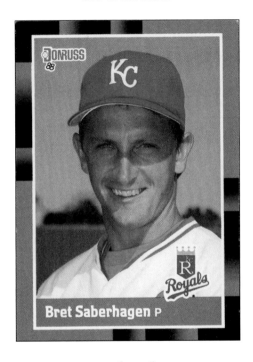

Bret Saberhagen
1988 Donruss
$1

Tim Salmon
2003 Upper Deck Vintage
$1

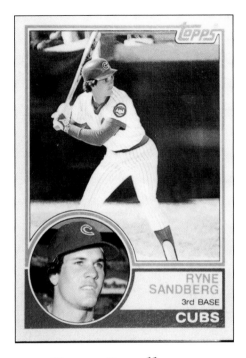

Ryne Sandberg
1983 Topps Rookie Card
$8

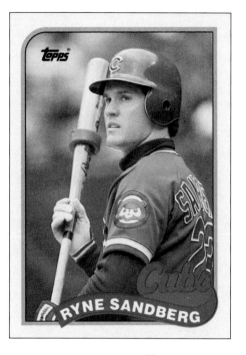

Ryne Sandberg
1989 Topps
$1

Baseball Card Field Guide

Ron Santo
1964 Topps
$14

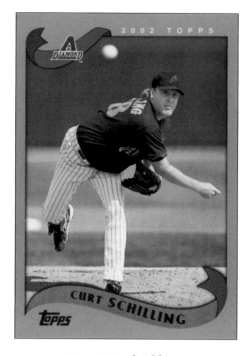

Curt Schilling
2002 Topps
$1

Baseball Card Field Guide

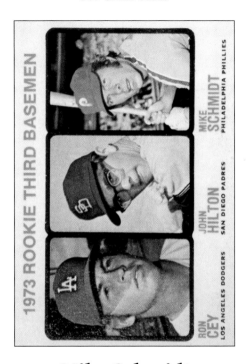

Mike Schmidt
1973 Topps Rookie Card
$95

PHILADELPHIA   3rd BASE

MIKE
SCHMIDT   PHILLIES

Mike Schmidt
1974 Topps
$20

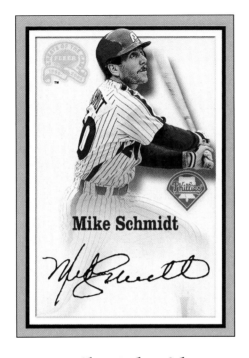

Mike Schmidt
2000 Fleer Greats of the Game Autograph
$300

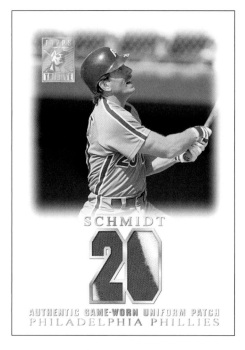

Mike Schmidt

2001 Topps Tribute Retired Jersey Number Relic

$50

Red Schoendienst
1956 Topps
$35

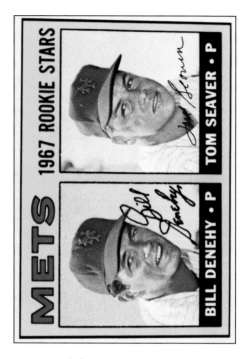

Tom Seaver
1967 Topps Rookie Card
$330

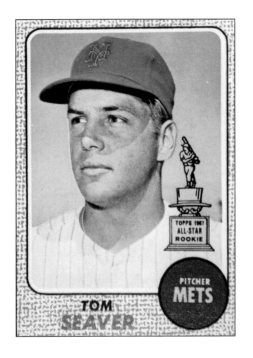

Tom Seaver
1968 Topps
$30

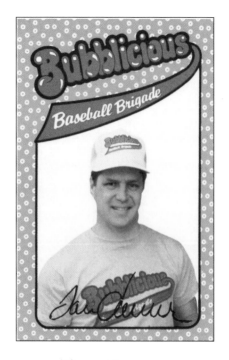

Tom Seaver
1987 Bubblicious Baseball Brigade
$65

Richie Sexson

1995 Bowman's Best Rookie Card

$12

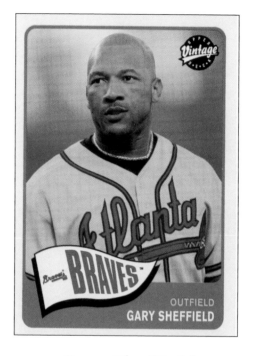

Gary Sheffield
2003 Upper Deck Vintage
$1

Gary Sheffield

2001 Upper Deck Sweet Spot Signatures

$30

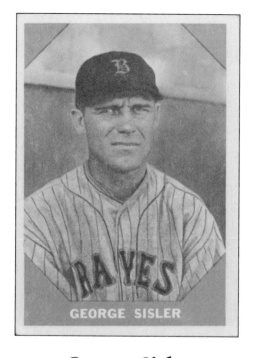

George Sisler
1960 Fleer Baseball Greats
$5

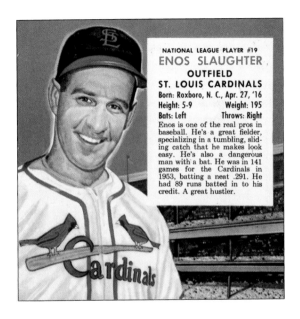

NATIONAL LEAGUE PLAYER #19
ENOS SLAUGHTER
OUTFIELD
ST. LOUIS CARDINALS
Born: Roxboro, N. C., Apr. 27, '16
Height: 5-9   Weight: 195
Bats: Left   Throws: Right
Enos is one of the real pros in
baseball. He's a great fielder,
specializing in a tumbling, slid-
ing catch that he makes look
easy. He's also a dangerous
man with a bat. He was in 141
games for the Cardinals in
1953, batting a neat .291. He
had 89 runs batted in to his
credit. A great hustler.

Enos Slaughter
1954 Red Man Tobacco
$135

Ozzie Smith
1979 Topps Rookie Card
$24

Ozzie Smith
2001 Topps Tribute Game Bat
$35

John Smoltz
2002 Topps Gallery
$1

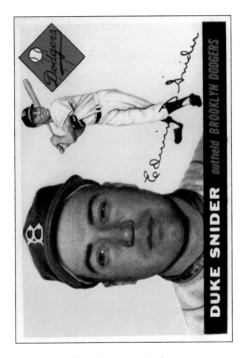

Duke Snider
1955 Topps
$480

DUKE SNIDER
OUTFIELDER—LOS ANGELES DODGERS

Duke Snider
1960 Leaf
$35

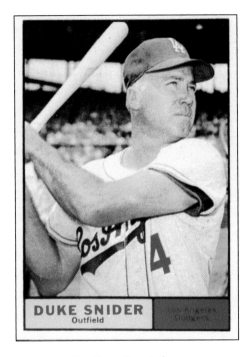

DUKE SNIDER
Outfield

Los Angeles
Dodgers

Duke Snider
1961 Topps
$23

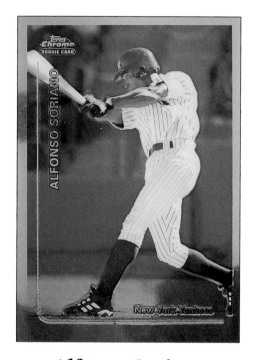

Alfonso Soriano
1999 Topps Chrome Traded Rookie Card
$15

Alfonso Soriano
1999 Bowman Chrome Rookie Card
$40

SAMMY SOSA OF

Sammy Sosa
1990 Leaf Rookie Card
$40

Sammy Sosa
2001 Donruss (1999 Diamond King)
$10

Sammy Sosa

2002 Bowman Heritage

$2

Sammy Sosa
2003 Bazooka Comics
$1

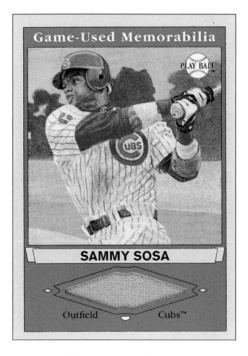

Sammy Sosa
2003 Upper Deck Play Ball Game Jersey
$15

Sosa/Griffey/Giambi

2003 SP Authentic Triple Chirography Autographs

$180

ROYAL STARS OF BASEBALL No. 5

WARREN SPAHN

The Boston Braves' southpaw pitcher was born in Buffalo, N. Y., April 23, 1921. He is 6 feet tall, weighs 175.

Spahn wound up the '49 season with 21 W., 14 L. He won most games; completed most games, 25; pitched most innings, 302; faced most batsmen, 1,258; led in strike-outs, 151. In 1947, he led League pitchers in earned-runs average, 2.33; most innings pitched, 290; and most shut-outs, 7.

Send for a Plastic Album to Hold Your Royal Stars Collection!

Eight clear envelopes, bound with colorful cover; displays 16 photo-graphs. Mail 15¢ and 3 Royal Desserts package fronts to Royal, Box 89, New York 46, N. Y.

Warren Spahn
1950 Royal Desserts
$200

Warren Spahn
1963 Topps
$35

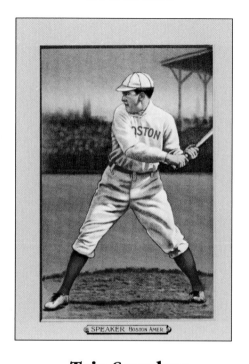

Tris Speaker
1911 Turkey Red Cabinets
$3,000

Willie Stargell
1964 Topps
$24

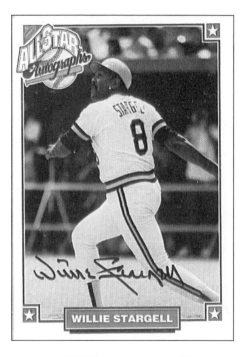

WILLIE STARGELL

Willie Stargell

1993 Nabisco All-Star Autographs

$15

Rusy Staub
1969 Topps
$3

CASEY STENGEL
MANAGER
NEW YORK YANKEES
Born: Kansas City, Mo., July 30, '91
Height: 5-10   Weight: 175
One of baseball's most humor-
ous and colorful men, as well
as one of its ablest. In his three
seasons as manager of the
Yankees, 1949, 1950 and 1951,
he has won three American
League pennants and three
World Championships. His base-
ball career goes back to 1910.
An outfielder, he played for 5
major league teams. Managing
since 1925. Also led Dodgers
and Braves.

Casey Stengel
1952 Red Man Tobacco
$55

Casey Stengel
1965 Topps
$5

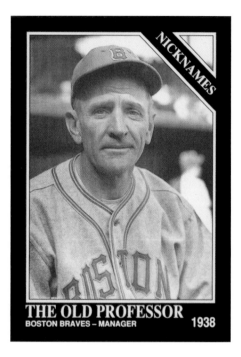

NICKNAMES

THE OLD PROFESSOR 1938
BOSTON BRAVES – MANAGER

Casey Stengel
1991-95 Conlon Collection
$1

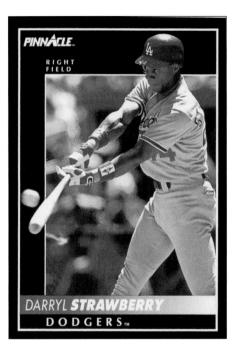

Darryl Strawberry
1992 Pinnacle
$1

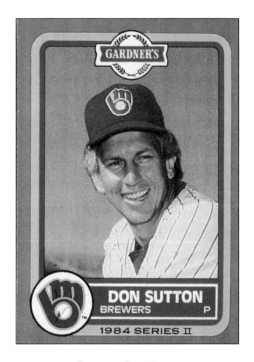

Don Sutton

1984 Gardner's Brewers

$1

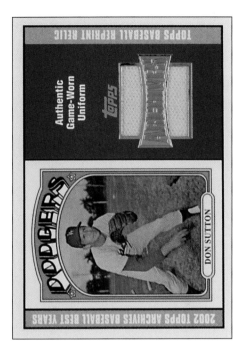

Don Sutton
2002 Topps Archives Game Jersey
$1

Ichiro Suzuki

2001 Upper Deck Ovation Rookie Card

$65

Ichiro Suzuki
2001 SPx Rookie Card
$450

Mark Teixeira

2001 Upper Deck Pros & Prospects Rookie Card

$80

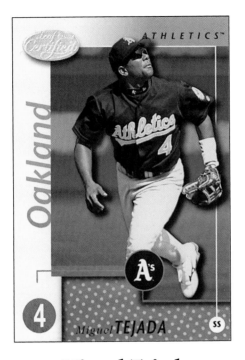

Miguel Tejada

2002 Leaf Certified

$2

Bill Terry
1960 Fleer Baseball Greats
$5

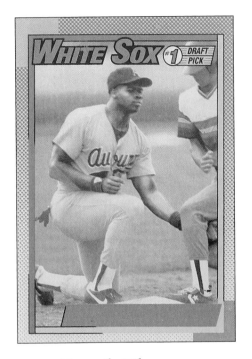

Frank Thomas
1990 Topps No-Name Variation
$450

FRANK THOMAS 1B

Frank Thomas
1990 Leaf Rookie Card
$12

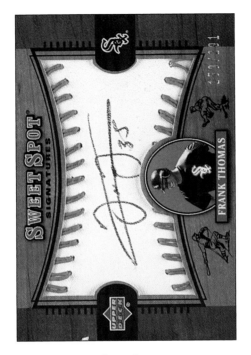

Frank Thomas
2002 Upper Deck Sweet Spot Signature
$50

Jim Thome
1992 Bowman
$1

Baseball Card Field Guide

Jim Thome
2001 Donruss Elite Aspirations
$10

ROYAL STARS OF BASEBALL No. 10

BOBBY THOMSON

Native of Glasgow, Scotland (Oct. 25, 1923), Thomson is one of the few European-born major leaguers. He came to the U. S. when he was 2. The New York Giants' right-handed outfielder is 6' 3", weighs 190.

In 1949, Bobby hit .309, sixth highest average in the National League. He racked up 35 doubles, 9 triples, 27 homers, 109 runs batted in. Only 2 other players in the League topped his 198 hits.

Send for a Plastic Album to Hold Your Royal Stars Collection!

Eight clear envelopes, bound with colorful cover; displays 16 photographs. Mail 15¢ and 3 Royal Desserts package fronts to Royal, Box 89, New York 46, N. Y.

Bobby Thomson
1950 Royal Desserts
$55

Bobby Thomson
1956 Topps
$25

Joe Torre
1962 Topps Rookie Card
$50

Baseball Card Field Guide

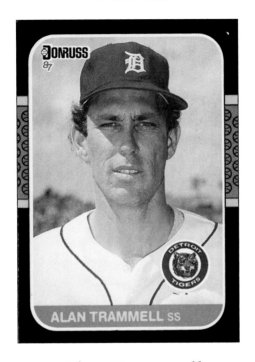

Alan Trammell

1987 Donruss

$1

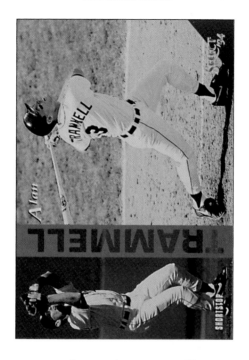

Alan Trammell

1994 Score Select

$1

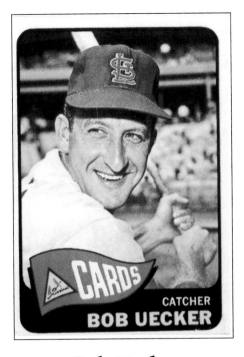

Bob Uecker
1965 Topps
$25

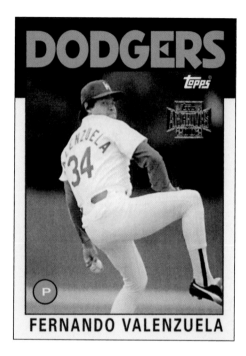

Fernando Valenzuela

2002 Topps Archives (1986 Topps replica)

$1

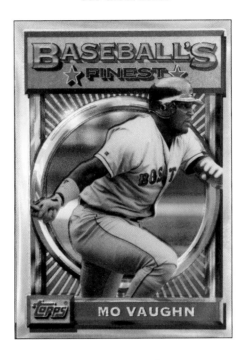

Mo Vaughn

1993 Topps Finest

$1

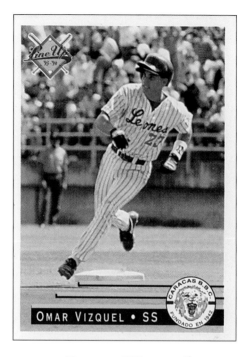

OMAR VIZQUEL • SS

Omar Vizquel
1993 Line Up Venezuelan Baseball
$1

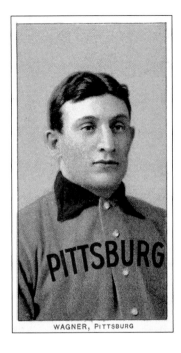

WAGNER, PITTSBURG

Honus Wagner
1909 T206 White Borders
$640,000

"HONUS" WAGNER

Honus Wagner
1940 Play Ball
$280

Honus Wagner
2002 Topps T206
$3

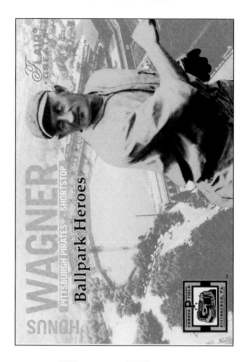

Honus Wagner
2003 Fleer Flair Greats Ballpark Heroes
$3

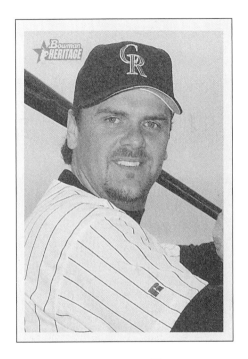

Larry Walker
2001 Bowman Heritage
$1

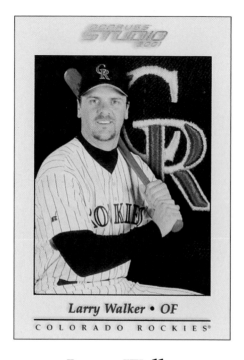

Larry Walker • OF

COLORADO ROCKIES®

Larry Walker
2001 Donruss Studio

$**1**

Buck Weaver
1912 T207 Brown Background
$1,225

ORIOLES
earl weaver • manager

Earl Weaver
2001 Topps Archives (1971 Topps)
$1

Vernon Wells
1997 Bowman Chrome Rookie Card
$12

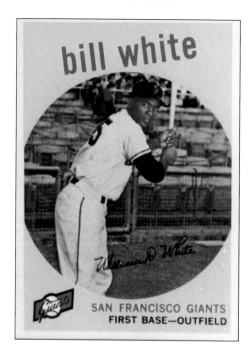

Bill White
1959 Topps
$13

Hoyt Wilhelm
1963 Topps
$11

Ted Williams
1954 Topps No. 250
$545

Ted Williams
1956 Topps
$475

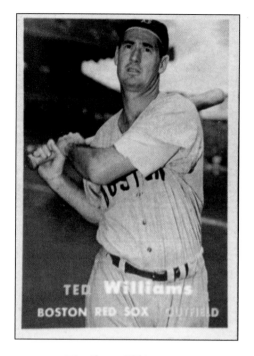

Ted Williams
1957 Topps
$325

Jan. 23, 1959 — Ted Signs For 1959

Ted Williams
1959 Fleer Ted Williams
$575

Bernie Williams
2002 Topps
$1

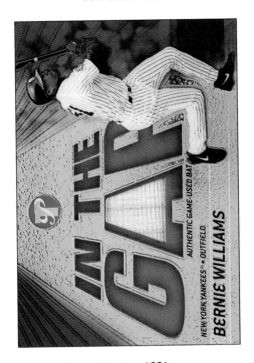

Bernie Williams
2002 Topps Pristine In The Gap Bat Card
$15

Billy Williams
1964 Topps
$15

Dontrelle Willis

2002 Bowman Chrome Draft Picks Rookie Card

$15

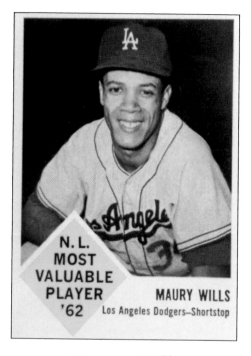

N. L.
MOST
VALUABLE
PLAYER
'62

MAURY WILLS
Los Angeles Dodgers–Shortstop

Maury Wills
1963 Fleer
$55

Maury Wills
1967 Topps
$95

Hack Wilson
1933 Goudey
$445

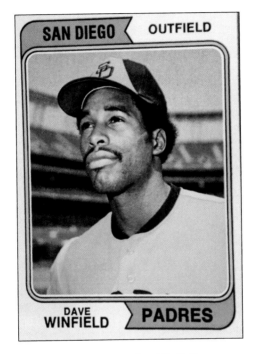

Dave Winfield
1974 Topps Rookie Card
$23

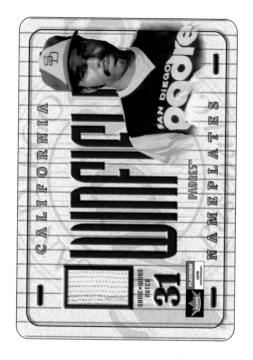

Dave Winfield

2001 Fleer Platinum Nameplates Jersey Card

$20

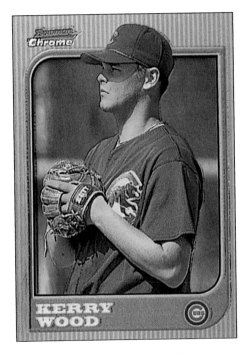

Kerry Wood
1997 Bowman Chrome Rookie Card
$15

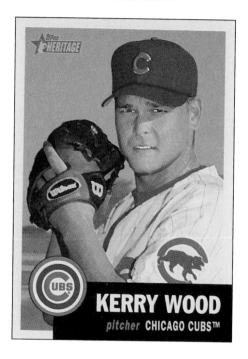

Kerry Wood
2002 Topps Heritage
$1

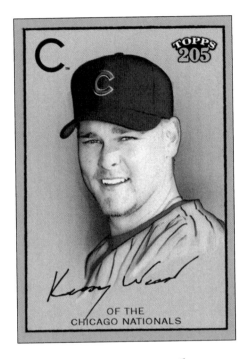

Kerry Wood
2003 Topps T205
$1

EARLY WYNN
pitcher CLEVELAND INDIANS

Early Wynn
1953 Topps
$70

Carl Yastrzemski
1965 Topps
$36

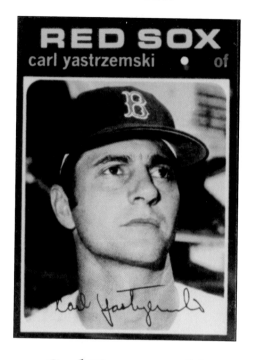

Carl Yastrzemski
1971 Topps
$21

"CY" YOUNG CLEVELAND

Cy Young
1911 T3 Turkey Red Cabinets
$3,000

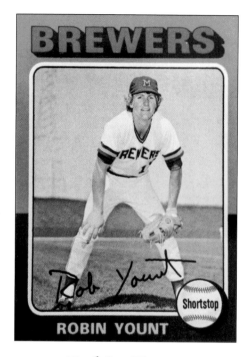

Robin Yount
1975 Topps Rookie Card
$23

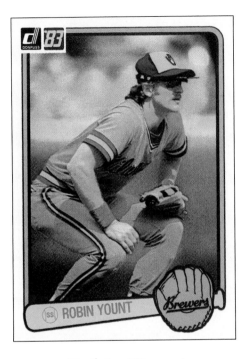

Robin Yount
1983 Donruss
$2

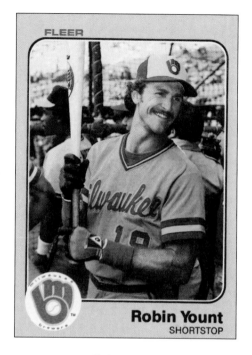

Robin Yount
1983 Fleer
$1

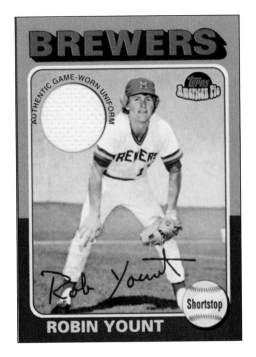

Robin Yount
2001 Topps American Pie Rookie Reprint Relics
$20

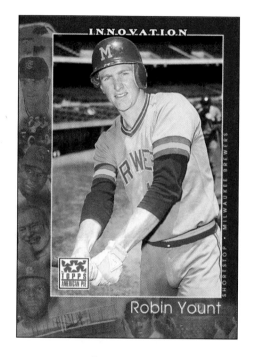

Robin Yount

2002 Topps American Pie Spirit of America

$1

DON
ZIMMER

CIN. REDS   3 BASE

Don Zimmer
1962 Topps
$9

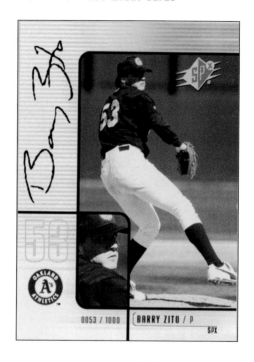

Barry Zito

2000 Upper Deck Rookie Update SP^X Rookie Autograph

$65